M000229512

365
Days
of
Gratitude

BroadStreet
PUBLISHING

BroadStreet Publishing Group, LLC.
Savage, Minnesota, USA
Broadstreetpublishing.com

365 Days of Gratitude

978-1-4245-6382-1
978-1-4245-6383-8 (eBook)

Devotional entries composed by Sara Perry.

Design and typesetting | garborgdesign.com
Editorial services by Sarah Eral and Michelle Winger | literallyprecise.com

Printed in China.

21 22 23 24 25 26 27   7 6 5 4 3 2 1

Let love and kindness be the motivation
behind all that you do.

1 CORINTHIANS 16:14 TPT

Introduction

We can walk in gratitude every day when we rely on God to be our source. When we focus on what we are grateful for, our satisfaction in life increases. Comparisons cease. Unnecessary pursuits pause. And we begin to notice the little things. The things that matter. Life. Breath. Generosity. Beauty. Grace. This is where we find deep connection with God.

As you read these devotions and Scriptures, be inspired to live with gratitude in your heart and praise on your lips. Meditate on things that produce life and peace. Evaluate each day in the light of God's truth and stand in awe of a heavenly Father who gives abundantly more than you can ask or imagine. As you quiet yourself before him, experience the goodness of his presence and be refreshed with his lifegiving joy.

Have an attitude of gratitude every day and watch how your perspective on life changes for the better.

January

Always give thanks to Father God
for every person he brings into your life
in the name of our Lord Jesus Christ.

EPHESIANS 5:20 TPT

Reason to Celebrate

Celebrate with praises the God and Father of our Lord Jesus Christ, who has shown us his extravagant mercy. For his fountain of mercy has given us a new life—we are reborn to experience a living, energetic hope through the resurrection of Jesus Christ from the dead.

1 PETER 1:3 TPT

The greatest reason we will ever have to celebrate is the beautiful and generous gift of God's mercy. He is full of more love than we can imagine, renewing and refreshing us daily in waves of his great grace. He sets us free from the cycles of sin and shame that keep us from living in the liberty of his lavish love.

Today is a new day, full of reasons to celebrate! The hope that has called you from the ashes of your despair is living and active; it is no stale idea. Just as Jesus rose from the grave and ascended to his Father, so has he raised you up in new spirit life. His power has broken every chain of sin and death, and he is your victory and living hope!

Praise the Lord for how he has met you with his tangible mercy.

Compassionate Comfort

Praise be to the God and Father
of our Lord Jesus Christ,
the Father of compassion
and the God of all comfort.

2 CORINTHIANS 1:3 NIV

God is not offended by our bad days. He can handle our low moments and our doubts. He is not surprised by our weakness. He is the God who stoops down in the dirt and gets close to us. He picks us up when we have no strength to lift ourselves. He is our constant help and forever friend. He is close in compassion, and he is near in comfort.

When we struggle to name our feelings, when we don't know how to make a hard day better, God is tender toward us. He does not require us to fake it. There is no need to pretend that we are surer than we are. We don't need to spin our realities for his sake. In his nearness, there is comfort. He sees us, and he knows our hearts. Let that be enough to turn toward him in gratitude.

Recognize that you are not alone in anything you face.

Divine Help

His divine power has granted to us all things that pertain to life and godliness, through the knowledge of him who called us to his own glory and excellence.

2 PETER 1:3 ESV

According to this verse, we have all we need in the Holy Spirit within us to empower us to live for Jesus. What he has called us to, he has provided. Everything we need is found in him! When we are running out of patience, he has it in spades. When we don't know what to do or where to turn, he has wisdom to guide us along the path of his love. Where we see only problems, he has solutions.

Instead of trying to get by on our own strength, we have the extraordinary presence of God with us to help us in all things. Let us not lean on our own understanding; let's press into the knowledge of him who has called us. We need look no further than Jesus. He is our greatest example, and he is our present help.

When you are faced with your own limitations,
turn to Jesus for help.

Commemorate Growth

We ought always to thank God for you, brothers and sisters, and rightly so, because your faith is growing more and more, and the love all of you have for one another is increasing.

2 Thessalonians 1:3 niv

While we are growing up, we achieve many milestones. When a baby takes its first steps, the parents rejoice in their child's growth. When a child learns how to ride their bike without training wheels, they practically burst with pride from the accomplishment! As they grow and become more independent, they breeze past many more landmarks.

In faith, we are like growing children. May we recognize and celebrate the indicators of our development. When we choose to offer loving presence instead of harsh opinion, we are showing maturity. When we believe that God will faithfully follow through on his promises to us, we are increasing in the strength of our trust. Every breakthrough is worth celebrating! May we look for ways to encourage one another in faith and in love.

When you recognize growth in someone,
point it out and celebrate with them!

Thankful for Others

You know that I've been called to serve the God of my fathers with a clean conscience. Night and day I pray for you, thanking God for your life!

2 TIMOTHY 1:3 TPT

In life, there are people we meet that stick with us. Though we may not see them as often as we hope, there is a bond that cannot be broken by time and distance. They are the ones we call on late nights, the ones we depend on in moments of stress and devastation. They are the ones who listen to us, support us, and who show up when it matters. And we do the same for them.

Have you ever gone through a season of life where you do not know what you would have done without the support of a trusted friend or family member? Does your heart not grow in gratitude thinking of how their presence made a difference for you? These people are gifts to us, grace wrapped up in relationship. What a beautiful picture of God's love they are!

Reach out to someone you love today and let them know how thankful you are for them!

Held Together

The Son is the dazzling radiance of God's splendor, the exact expression of God's true nature—his mirror image! He holds the universe together and expands it by the mighty power of his spoken word. He accomplished for us the complete cleansing of sins, and then took his seat on the highest throne at the right hand of the majestic One.

HEBREWS 1:3 TPT

God is a mystery to us. We have not seen him face to face, and he is far greater than our understanding can grasp. However, we can clearly see his nature through Jesus. The character of Jesus, the Son of God, is the exact likeness of the character of God the Father. What is more, the Spirit reveals to us in even more depth the reality of the nature of God's love.

Jesus revealed God as our loving Father. He is not looking for perfection from us but humble surrender. He is patient with us in our weakness, he is generous with his mercy, and he does not want to lose any of us to cycles of sin and shame. He has provided all that we need to live in the freedom of his love. He is the source, and he is our great Savior and reward. It all stems from him!

*Surrender your heart to the Father of love
and thank him for his mercy.*

Reliable Friends

Every time I think of you,
I give thanks to my God.

PHILIPPIANS 1:3 NLT

What does it look like to be a reliable friend? Are we people who others can count on in times of need and times of celebration? In the experience of loyal relationships, we are able to catch glimpses of God's faithful love toward us. When we live with love as our banner, extending mercy to others whenever we have the opportunity, we reflect the heart of our good Father.

Are there people in your life that you can count on, no matter what? They are treasured gifts from God. Friends who fight for us when we have no strength of our own, who support us in our endeavors, who show up when we need them, and whom we can be completely ourselves with, are a blessing. May we be people who are reliable in love, and may we reach out with intention.

Thank God for your trusted friends!

Great Expectation

It is by his great mercy that we have been born again....
Now we live with great expectation, and we have a
priceless inheritance—an inheritance that is kept in
heaven for you, pure and undefiled, beyond the reach of
change and decay.

1 PETER 1:3-4 NLT

By the great mercy of Jesus, we have been ushered into
the freedom of his kingdom. We have been born again into
a family—the family of God. Our great expectation, our
wonderful hope, is not in what we can achieve or acquire
on this earth. It is the overwhelmingly costly inheritance of
eternal life.

When we look ahead to the coming of Christ's kingdom
in its fullness, we set our eyes on things above. It does not
mean that we must escape the realities of our lives, for
God is with us through his Spirit to help, transform, and
encourage us in the midst of every crisis. As we turn our
attention to God's unfailing love and his faithful nature,
may our hearts find hope in the promise of his coming
unsurpassable goodness.

When you are overwhelmed today,
remember that troubles are fleeting.
Turn your attention to God's faithful promises.

Precious Promises

He has granted to us his precious and very great promises, so that through them you may become partakers of the divine nature, having escaped from the corruption that is in the world because of sinful desire.

2 PETER 1:4 ESV

With faithfulness, God remains the same in unchanging love. He who is loyal to his word continues to follow through on his promises. He will not forget a single one! God is not a man that he would lie; there is no room for deceit or manipulation in his gracious mercy. He is full of truth, integrity, and follow-through. He is perfect in all of his ways, and we can trust him completely.

He will do what he has said he will. Perhaps you find yourself in a waiting season between promise and fulfillment. The in-between is where endurance keeps you tethered to his love. God will not fail. He is with you in your longing, and he is with you in the satisfaction of realized hopes.

*Take time to remember God's faithfulness
to you and others.*

Gracious Generosity

I thank God because in Christ you have been made rich in every way, in all your speaking and in all your knowledge.

1 CORINTHIANS 1:5 NCV

When our words drip with kindness and our knowledge promotes the wisdom of Christ, we reflect the generosity of God's love within us. He does not withhold his wisdom from those who ask for it. Jesus does not turn us away in our pursuit of his powerful presence. His leadership keeps us on the path of his humble mercy. We reveal the fruit of his Spirit, working in us to transform our lives into his image, as we continually submit to his ways.

A kind word spoken at the right time can diffuse the defensive nature of an argument. The wisdom of Jesus is full of the promotion of peace, unity, and love. When we listen with compassion and respond with thoughtfulness, the wealth of Christ's wisdom is made evident. May we be people who reflect the loving nature of our Savior in every conversation.

Give another the benefit of compassion and kindness, remembering this is how God relates to you.

Only Light

This is the message we have heard from him
and declare to you: God is light;
in him there is no darkness at all.

1 JOHN 1:5 NIV

When we walk through long, dark nights of the soul, it can be hard to remember what the ease of sunny days felt like. We cannot escape suffering in this life, and we can't outrun loss. We will find ourselves in the pit of grief at some point, no matter how graciously we live. Loss is not a punishment to us. Jesus experienced it himself. There is solace in his presence, for he knows what we go through. He knows the ache of sorrow, and he is with us in it.

Though mourning may last for a season of night, there is the promise of a new day of rejoicing ahead. In the light of his radiance, we will see what we could not in the darkness of our grief. We will see the seeds that were sown in sorrow springing up into gardens of beautiful new life. He does not waste a thing. He is light, and in him there is no darkness. He sees everything clearly, and he does not miss a single detail.

*Trust that God sees what you cannot
and ask him for his perspective today.*

Given a Family

God decided in advance to adopt us into his own family by bringing us to himself through Jesus Christ. This is what he wanted to do, and it gave him great pleasure.

EPHESIANS 1:5 NLT

No matter how loving your family is, there are bound to be areas of frustration, as well as needs that have gone unmet. On the other hand, no matter how dysfunctional your family system may have been, there is a place where you belong. Through Jesus, you have been brought into God's family. You are his beloved child, and he loves you perfectly and completely, just as you are.

There's no need to prove your worth to your good Father. He sees you as you are, and he completely accepts you. He sees you through the lens of Jesus, full of love and mercy. You don't have to dress yourself up, and you don't have to earn your place. He knows you, and he draws you to his heart with gentle kindness. He is fierce in love, breaking down the lies and walls of shame that you keep you at a distance. Come, find your place at his table today. You are a part of his family!

Come to the Father with an open heart
to receive from his abundant love.

Simply Ask

If any of you is lacking in wisdom,
ask God, who gives to all generously and ungrudgingly,
and it will be given you.

JAMES 1:5 NRSV

There is no need to hesitate in God's presence. He always gives freely and generously from his heart of mercy to all who come to him. Instead of reasoning your way out of your requests, present them all to him without censorship. He wants you as you are, not how you think you should come. Nothing you say can surprise him, and he is absolutely unoffendable.

What a reason to be thankful today, that God wants you, all of you, without exception. You need not fear his response. Don't self-protect by withholding your heart from him. He is faithful to meet you with the overflow of his affection. He loves you more than you realize and more than you could hope. Throw off your inhibitions and enter into his presence with praise and thanksgiving.

Give God access to all your thoughts and feelings.
He cares for you!

Deeply Understood

"Before I formed you in the womb I knew you,
before you were born I set you apart."

JEREMIAH 1:5 NIV

When you feel misunderstood by others, rest in the
assurance that you are completely known by God. He does
not mistake your intentions, and he knows every move of
your heart. He created you with purpose, and he knit you
together with love. He knows all of your quirks and your
talents. He delights in your joy, and he never misinterprets
your words.

When you try your best but fail to meet the expectations
of others, there is no reason to hide in shame. Let it be
an opportunity for humble love to lead you. You are not
perfect, and you cannot please everyone. You can extend
kindness and mercy toward others while filling up on the
source of life itself. Let your identity be rooted in who God
says you are, not in the opinion of others.

*Practice self-acceptance where you are prone to shaming
yourself, and let God speak his truth over your identity.*

Confident in Christ

I am confident of this very thing,
that He who began a good work in you
will perfect it until the day of Christ Jesus.

PHILIPPIANS 1:6 NASB

When disappointment meets you, what is your response?
Are you prone to wallowing in self-pity or catastrophizing
the future? If this is your go-to, know that there is grace for
you in every single moment. Grace to empower you in the
power of God's Spirit. Grace that is abundant and able to
transform you and give you strength in your weakness.

Instead of relying on your own ability to grow, you get to
lean on the confidence of Christ, who is in you, to perfect
you in every single way. There is no need to strive for his
love and acceptance. You already have it! Stand strong on
the Word of the Lord that set you free from the chains of
sin and shame. Perfectionism is not the goal; dependence
on the Perfect One is!

Lean on the confidence of Christ
over your own abilities today.

Pure Light of Unity

If we keep living in the pure light that surrounds him,
we share unbroken fellowship with one another, and
the blood of Jesus, his Son, continually cleanses us
from all sin.

1 JOHN 1:7 TPT

When we live in the freedom of Christ's love, gratitude is sown like seeds into the soil of our lives. If we have been forgiven much, how much more will we forgive others? When we look through the perspective of Jesus, who makes all things new, our faith is strengthened in the endless possibilities of his restorative power.

Instead of going mindlessly through our day, may we be aware of the tangible grace of God with us. He shines on us with his glorious presence. In the light of his nearness, we can see others more clearly, too. May we reach out in love to those who bear his image. Let us not get caught up on the divisive issues that drive us further from each other. Instead, let's be united in purpose and heart through his love.

When you feel criticism rising within you,
ask God for his perspective.

Lighthearted Joy

Your hearts can soar with joyful gratitude when you think of how God made you worthy to receive the glorious inheritance freely given to us by living in the light.

COLOSSIANS 1:12 TPT

When was the last time you considered the amazing gift of God's favor through Christ Jesus? Have you forgotten the deep joy of knowing that you are completely covered by the love of Jesus? He has set you free, calling you into the abundance of life in the glorious light of his mercy.

Take a few moments now to think through the impact of his love on your life. You have been chosen by the King of kings to know him! You have been adopted into his family, and he calls you his own. He has given you his Spirit to dwell within you and teach, strengthen, guide, and empower you. There is so much more to discover in his vast affection than you have yet tasted. Let your heart rejoice in this reality!

Thank God for the freedom you have in Jesus.

Tools for Living

God will never give you the spirit of fear,
but the Holy Spirit who gives you mighty power,
love, and self-control.

2 TIMOTHY 1:7 TPT

God does not deal with us in shame or fear. He guides us gently, his firm hand holding ours. He does not drive us with threats. We need no further look than his Spirit for help with how to live. We do not need to go to the ends of the earth, or even the end of our street, to find him. He is here with us now, in power and in presence.

The Holy Spirit gives us strength in our weakness, strategies for our problems, wisdom for our questions, loving acceptance, and kind correction. He moves with compassion and mercy, and he delivers us from our fears. He is peace personified, comforter in our sorrows, and he is pure love. He moves in the same resurrection power that raised Christ from the grave. He is our constant help and our forever advocate. May we never lose sight of the incredible power that is God with us.

*Look for where love rings loudly
over the cries of fear around you.*

Abundantly Kind

He is so rich in kindness and grace that he purchased our freedom with the blood of his Son and forgave our sins.

EPHESIANS 1:7 NLT

The nature of God is unmistakably good. He is better than we are in all ways. He is more patient with us than we are with others or even ourselves. He is full of compassion when we run out of it. He is able to deal with the realities of our circumstances without being worried or anxious. He meets us with mercy, draws us in with kindness, and loves us to life over and over again.

When we need a reminder of God's loving character, let us look to the life of Jesus and remember that he is the living expression of the Father. He did not exclude the vulnerable from his message of peace with God. He spent time with those the religious elite shunned. He healed the sick, made blind eyes see, and raised the dead to life again. He set the tormented free. Everything he did was driven by the merciful kindness of God. He remains the same today.

Be intentional in kindness to others today.

Help in All Things

The Lord is good,
a refuge in times of trouble.
He cares for those who trust in him.

NAHUM 1:7 NIV

What a beautiful God is the Lord! He is the Good Shepherd, taking care of his flock at all times. He keeps a watchful eye over them, and he leaves the ninety-nine to rescue the one who wanders off. He sees us in our trouble, and he offers us his help. He tenderly cares for those who trust in him. He will not ever abandon us in our distress.

The Lord is a strong and mighty shelter. His peace goes beyond our logic to fill our souls with his very near presence. When we are worried, let us turn to him. When fear has us responding in fight or flight, may our warrior God rise up on our behalf! He will keep us secure in his love; nothing can ever separate us from his mercy. He is our skillful and ready relief.

When you are worried or overwhelmed,
find refuge in the presence of God and give thanks.

Inexpressible Glory

Though you have not seen Him, you love Him, and though you do not see Him now, but believe in Him, you greatly rejoice with joy inexpressible and full of glory.

1 PETER 1:8 NASB

We do not have to wait for everything to be made clear in order to experience the deep joy of God's promises. Though we have not yet seen him, we love him. He has revealed his glorious nature all around us! His mercy no one can fault. His wisdom is unmatched. He is the way, the truth, and the life, and he is the source of all good gifts.

May today be the day we rejoice in our great God and King. Let us remember his faithfulness through the ages and be encouraged at his unchanging character. He is still the same God who delivered the Israelites from their captivity. He is the one who heals, restores, and revives. He is the source of life, and he is inexpressibly good.

Thank God for the glimpses you have seen of his glory. Pour out your love to him.

Firm Foundation

"I am the Alpha and the Omega," says the LORD God,
"who is, and who was, and who is to come,
the Almighty."

REVELATION 1:8 NIV

God is so much greater than any circumstance we face in this life. He is bigger than our small lives can contain. His reach is larger than the farthest universe, yet he knows us intimately. He is beyond our understanding, yet he is so very near. The earth is a footstool to him. No mind can comprehend how vast he is, and his power no one can fathom.

This is the God who calls us each by name. This is our firm foundation and our hope. We are not pawns in a game that he is playing. We are objects of his affection, and he is faithful to fulfill every promise that he has made. He does not shift or change from loyal love. We only see in very small part, but he doesn't miss a detail in the vast expanse of creation. Let us look to him and throw our hope into the ocean of his love.

*Put your problems into perspective
by reflecting on God's greatness.*

Faithful to Forgive

If we confess our sins, He is faithful and just to forgive us our sins and to cleanse us from all unrighteousness.

1 JOHN 1:9 ESV

Though none of us is perfect in love, God is. He forgives when we confess our secret shames to him. He throws our sins into the sea of forgetfulness and does not hold them against us. Though we cannot escape the repercussions of how our choices affect others, and the consequences that come as a result, we can know that we are not defined by our mistakes.

In the pure love of Jesus, we are made clean. What he does not hold against us, let us not hold against each other. This does not mean that there is no accountability. Where others have offended us, let us forgive them so that the root of bitterness will not have a hold in our hearts. God's love is strong enough for truth, justice, and mercy to reign together.

Confess your sin, let go of your shame,
and walk in the freedom of God's forgiveness.

Holy Hope

He delivered us from such a deadly peril,
and he will deliver us.
On him we have set our hope
that he will deliver us again.

2 CORINTHIANS 1:10 ESV

Jesus is our great deliverer. What he has done already, he will do again. Let us look with hope to the future, knowing that the one who was revealed as rescuer and Savior will be our advocate and help. He does not grow tired of helping us when we need him. He does not turn us away when we come to him for assistance.

In our hour of great need, let us come to Jesus, our deliverer. In times of stress, let's look to him for aid. Whatever it is that upsets us, he cares about it. In everything, we can confidently come before him, knowing he welcomes us with open arms. He will not turn away from us, for he is faithful in love, and he does not abandon his people.

Give Jesus your worries.
Let his faithful love be your confidence.

Welcomed In

He has delivered us from the power of darkness and conveyed us into the kingdom of the Son of His love.

COLOSSIANS 1:13 NKJV

Have you ever felt out of place? Perhaps you joined a gym that felt intimidating, or you walked into a church where everyone seemed to know each other. Maybe you don't feel this at all. Maybe you feel this practically everywhere. No matter the case, you have a place where you belong. It is in the family of God, where he draws you in with open arms and welcomes you to a reserved place at his table.

No one else can take your place in his kingdom. You are unique, and you are irreplaceable to God, your Father. May you comprehend how deeply known you are and how fully accepted you are in him. There is nowhere else where you can be as freely yourself and loved so completely. May you know this deep, liberating love more and more with each new day.

Encourage someone today with something you appreciate about them.

Overflowing with Love

The Living Expression became a man and lived among us! And we gazed upon the splendor of his glory, the glory of the One and Only who came from the Father overflowing with tender mercy and truth!

JOHN 1:14 TPT

Jesus is the living expression of God the Father. His life dripped with kindness, his words with tender mercy and truth. Everything he did in his ministry was a reflection of the Father's heart. We see clearly through Jesus that mercy triumphs judgment. His love paved the way for us to know the Father and to worship him in spirit and in truth.

When we submit our lives to Christ, we let his mercy guide us. We cannot hold onto our pride and still walk the path of his love humbly. Let us throw off the things that entangle us and keep us from moving freely in his mercy. If love is the highest law, then let's live to its standard.

Look to Jesus for how to live in the example of his love.

Patience

Jesus Christ might display his perfect patience
as an example to those who were
to believe in him for eternal life.

1 TIMOTHY 1:16 ESV

In an age of instant answers, we have lost the beauty of the tension of the in-between. With patience comes endurance. Though we can look for, and find, quick answers to trivial questions, some problems aren't so readily solved. Along the journey of this life, we will either learn to wrestle with God in the tension or give up. May we be people of tenacity that choose to stay engaged with the Lord, even in our questioning.

In his perfect patience, Jesus leaves room for transformation and growth. In this space, there is the freedom to try and fail. There is opportunity to grow and learn. Let us not become discouraged as we discover new skills and find that it takes time to become proficient in them. Let us display patience and implement the values of Christ's kingdom as we transform more into his likeness.

*Instead of trying to fix something for others today,
practice patience and let them work it out.*

Remember Them

I have not stopped giving thanks for you,
remembering you in my prayers.

EPHESIANS 1:16 NIV

In life, there are people who forever change us and point us in a direction we would not have taken on our own. They are teachers who champion us, coaches who push us beyond our limits, and friends who encourage us. They are mentors who instruct us with the wisdom of their experience and who guide us with their advice.

Think back over your life. Whom has impacted you? Whom can you recognize as a voice of reason, truth, and encouragement? What a gift from God they are to you! Reflect on how they revealed the love of God to you in specific ways. Pray for the blessing that they have given you to be returned to them. Let the gratitude of your heart overflow with thanks to the Father as you honor the imprint that they have left on your life.

Reach out to someone who has impacted your life and express gratitude toward them.

Good News

Christ didn't send me to baptize, but to preach the Good News—and not with clever speech, for fear that the cross of Christ would lose its power.

1 CORINTHIANS 1:17 NLT

The good news of Jesus is not found in lofty language or complex thought. It is in the simple truth of the gospel. The cross of Christ is the basis of our salvation. Jesus' death and resurrection lead us to everlasting life, where the power of the grave has been broken. It is the grave-busting mercy of God that ushers us into the abundance of life in his kingdom.

The good news is life to those who are dying. It is healing to the sick, hope for the destitute, and freedom for the captive. It does not prop up powerful systems. The gospel of Jesus is freedom for all who look to him. It reaches the vulnerable as well as the firmly established. No one is excluded from his love. Let us revel in the good news of our great Savior, for he has made a way where there was none.

Share the good news of Jesus' love with someone today.

Glorious Inheritance

I pray that the eyes of your heart may be enlightened,
so that you will know what is the hope of His calling,
what are the riches of the glory of His inheritance
in the saints.

EPHESIANS 1:18 NASB

If living for Jesus was about impressing others, then it would fall flat as soon as trouble hit. The power of Christ is not in our understanding of Scriptures; it is in the living out of his love. The hope of our calling is not found in this world. There are glimpses of God's goodness in our lives, to be sure. But there is a much greater reality that we are living for.

In the kingdom of God, where all wrong things are made right and justice reigns, there is love that covers over every fault and flaw. We get to experience the kingdom of God as we surrender in the mercy of God and partner with him to bring heaven to earth. And yet, there is a far greater goodness that we will experience in the fullness of his kingdom when his throne is established for all to see. What a glorious inheritance we have now, and what fullness we have to look forward to!

Look to Jesus today for hope and inspiration.

Yes and Amen

All of God's promises have been fulfilled in Christ with a resounding "Yes!" And through Christ, our "Amen" ascends to God for his glory.

2 CORINTHIANS 1:20 NLT

Every promise that God has made is complete in Jesus. He is the pure image of God's love. He is both the yes and amen of all God's vows. What he has begun, he will continue to do until it is finished. There is not a single promise that does not find its fulfillment in Christ.

When we join our hearts in agreement with God's spoken Word, we add our amen to the chorus of those who have gone before us. There is power in partnering with the promises of God. When we stand on the foundation of others' faith, we will find our own bolstered. We will find our hearts stirred with hope as we recall the faithfulness of God through the ages. He is the same today, and he won't ever change.

Pray God's promises today and let your amen resound!

February

Enter his gates with thankgiving;
go into his courts with praise.
Give thanks to him and praise his name.

PSALM 100:4 NLT

Firm Faith

It is through him that you now believe in God, who raised him from the dead and glorified him, so that you would fasten your faith and hope in God alone.

1 PETER 1:21 TPT

Our faith is not dependent on what we do. It is not based on our abilities or skills. All of our hopes are firmly established in God. They are dependent on his faithfulness, and we know that he is loyal and true. No matter how much we have failed, God is unchanging in faithfulness. What a reason to celebrate today!

May you take a deep breath of relief as you let his greatness settle into your consciousness. Let go of what you cannot control. Trust that the Lord will continue to work all things together for his glory and for your good. He is a firm foundation to stand upon, and he is a safe place to rest.

Remember that God is more than able to do what you need him to do; trust him to do it!

Remain in Love

Keep yourselves in the love of God, waiting for the mercy of our Lord Jesus Christ that leads to eternal life.

JUDE 1:21 ESV

As we journey through this life, we have a myriad of opportunities to engage with others in love or distance ourselves in apathy. The choice is ours. When we look to the example of Jesus, we see how compassion compelled him to reach out to others. Love is more than an attitude; it is also an invitation. Love reconciles us to one another, and it covers a multitude of wrongs.

What does it look like to remain in the mercy of God? As we clothe ourselves in the compassion of Christ, we choose to humble ourselves instead of excusing our lack of kindness toward others. God's love is our source, our foundation, and our strength. We love because he first loved us, so let us draw from the deep springs of his affection.

Keep love at the forefront of your mind
as you go about your day.

Faultless

All glory to God, who is able to keep you from falling away and will bring you with great joy into his glorious presence without a single fault.

JUDE 1:24 NLT

What God does not hold against us, may we also not hold against ourselves. We are often our own harshest critics, holding ourselves to standards that are impossible to meet. We cannot be perfect. We will never get it all right. Can we give ourselves the permission to pursue growth without the need to be flawless? There is a difference between the pursuit of excellence and perfection; let's not confuse them.

Instead of reaching for the impossible, we can let go of the expectation of perfection. In God, we are given fresh starts as often as we need them. This doesn't mean that we escape the consequences of our choices, but it also doesn't confine us to our past. With gratitude, let's remember that God is the one who covers us, calls us, and perfects us in his love.

Forgive yourself as Christ has forgiven you.

God Is Better

The foolishness of God is wiser than human wisdom, and
the weakness of God is stronger than human strength.

1 CORINTHIANS 1:25 NIV

Though we face our limits on a daily basis, may we never
forget that God's strength is limitless. His wisdom is
superior to any knowledge that we can gain in this world.
We catch glimpses of beauty, and we know moments of
awe and wonder. Still, the greatness of God is far greater
than anything we have yet seen or could ever imagine.

Instead of relying on what we have today, may we press
into the presence of God for more of him. He has solutions
for our problems, power to help us endure our present
troubles, grace to give us space to grow, and more than
enough rest for our weary souls. Everything we long for is
found in him. He is the fulfillment of every need and every
desire. He gives good gifts, yet he is the greatest one of all.

*Remember God's goodness when you
are disappointed by others.*

Forgiveness Abounds

The next day he saw Jesus coming toward him and declared, "Here is the Lamb of God who takes away the sin of the world!"

JOHN 1:29 NRSV

There is nothing in this world that is too big for Jesus to handle. No war, no trauma, nothing. His sacrifice covers it all, and those who come to him are covered in his compassion. His mercy draws us in, and he purifies us in the overwhelming power of his love.

Is there something that you have been withholding from God? Is there an area of life that has been your secret struggle? Let his light shine on you as you bring him the good, the bad, and the ugly. He is full of power to lift you up from the pit that has trapped you. He is not surprised or offended by anything you present him with. Let him in and let him help you. He loves you more than you can imagine.

Be honest with God today about your struggles and embrace his forgiveness.

No One Like Him

"There is no one holy like the LORD, indeed, there is no one besides You, nor is there any rock like our God."

1 SAMUEL 2:2 NASB

It is not a small thing to look to Jesus in our trials and troubles. He is our life-source, our anchor of hope, and our firm foundation. When we look with the perspective of heaven, it is an eagle-eye view. What we cannot see from the ground level is clear from a higher vantage point.

May we see through the lens of Jesus today when we look at our lives. There is no detail that he misses. Everything is brought together with the thread of his marvelous mercy running through our lives. He has not left us to fend for ourselves. May we lean into the presence of God today and press in to hear his voice. He guides us in grace, and his steps are steady. He never falters, so let us be confident in his leadership.

Put your problems in the light of God's faithfulness.

Living for God

We speak as messengers approved by God
to be entrusted with the Good News.
Our purpose is to please God, not people.
He alone examines the motives of our hearts.

1 THESSALONIANS 2:4 NLT

The whims of this world shift as often as the winds do. It is impossible to please everyone with our lives, and this shouldn't be the goal. If we are looking to make others happy, we will find that we cannot achieve this, for others or for ourselves. As long as our purpose is driven by outside expectations, we will not be satisfied.

May you live with the purposes of God as your ultimate goal. May love be the driving force of your life. May his words of promise keep you going. He has given you everything you need to face every moment of your life, for he has given you himself. You have access to his kingdom wisdom, his gracious strength, and his overcoming love at all times. His presence is with you. Lean into his great affection today. Let it both fill and fuel you.

Examine whether you are seeking to please people or God with your choices.

Covered by Love

He has brought me to his banquet hall,
And his banner over me is love.

SONG OF SOLOMON 2:4 NASB

When we come to God through Jesus, we are welcomed into the great banquet hall of his kingdom. He has reserved a place for each of us, and no one else can take it. There is a table overflowing with rich foods to nourish us. There are no hidden motives in his heart. There is only love.

Will you lay aside the endless demands you put on yourself today and give yourself a few minutes to simply soak in the love of God? There is no striving in it. A dearly loved child knows that they don't have to perform for their parent's affection. So it is with you and your good Father. He delights in you, not for what you offer him but for who you are. Let that sink in today as you look to him.

Confidently approach God in prayer today,
knowing that love ushers you in.

Trust and Obey

If anyone obeys his word, love for God is truly made complete in them. This is how we know we are in him.

1 John 2:5 NIV

When we truly trust God, it is more than sitting back and waiting for him to act on our behalf. We partner with him as he moves us in his love. We prove our faith when we live it out. If we claim to love God and to follow him, then our lives will reflect it.

The path of love that Jesus laid out is narrow, and not many choose to take it. Is that because it is exclusive? By no means! Few choose to follow the path of laid-down love because it requires humility, letting go of our offenses, and extending mercy instead of vengeance. When we follow him along the pathway of his peace, we no longer have the right to throw stones at anyone. May we live out the truth that Jesus has revealed, for his ways are better than our own.

Wait on God today and ask him to speak to you. Act on what he says.

Holy Habitation

You are living stones that God is building into his spiritual temple. What's more, you are his holy priests. Through the mediation of Jesus Christ, you offer spiritual sacrifices that please God.

1 Peter 2:5 NLT

We do not have to make a long trek or embark on a voyage to find God. He meets us where we are. What a wonderfully mysterious and indescribably good God he is! He makes his home with us. Jesus promised that when he left earth, the Father would send the Holy Spirit to never leave us.

The Holy Spirit is our advocate, our help, and our constant companion. Holy Spirit is our strength, our song, and our greatest source. Holy Spirit is God himself, and he is with us. Like the wind, we can see and sense how he moves. God is not bound to matter or to time, transcending it all as he makes himself at home in us who yield our lives to him. May we know the powerful and tangible presence of God in our lives, in our homes, and in our beings.

Thank God for his Holy Spirit that lives in you.

Endless Wisdom

The LORD grants wisdom!
From his mouth come knowledge and understanding.

PROVERBS 2:6 NLT

Though admitting our own limits may look like weakness and foolishness to the world, it is the beginning of wisdom. When we are able to honestly acknowledge that we don't have all the answers, we open ourselves to the wisdom that can expand our understanding. God is full of clarity, light, and life. In him, every mystery is resolved.

The Lord grants wisdom to all who seek it. He is not stingy with his revelations. When we ask him for guidance and for solutions, he will give it. A humble heart is teachable. There is no need to "fake it until you make it" with God. He isn't fooled by our platitudes or our presentations. He sees our hearts, and he knows us in our frailty. Let us yield to his leadership, for he always guides us in his perfect love and wisdom.

*Humble your heart before the Lord today
and ask for his perspective.*

Established in Mercy

Let your roots grow down into him, and let your lives be built on him. Then your faith will grow strong in the truth you were taught, and you will overflow with thankfulness.

COLOSSIANS 2:7 NLT

When we build our lives on Jesus and his kingdom, the foundation is sure and strong. His love is unshakable, and his peace is like a river flowing through the soil of our hearts. When our faith is built on Jesus, it will not be shaken. When it is built on our own abilities, however, it will surely crumble. If the faith we have is in the systems of this world, the foundation is already cracked. It will not hold up to time and pressure.

Let's examine where our trust truly lies. What are our greatest hopes in this life? What are the values that guide us? As we reflect on the underlying expectations of our hearts, may we align them with the kingdom of Jesus, knowing that his ways are better than our own. He is trustworthy, and he will not fail.

Make a list of the values that you want to live your life by.

Lifted from the Dust

"He raises the poor from the dust and lifts the needy from the ash heap; he seats them with princes and has them inherit a throne of honor. For the foundations of the earth are the LORD's; on them he has set the world."

1 SAMUEL 2:8 NIV

Our God is not disconnected from the reality of our hardship. He is not detached from our suffering. He is the God who gets down in the dirt of our circumstances and lifts us up from the rubble of our despair. He is the one who meets us in the midst of our mess.

Jesus is the one who showed us just how wonderfully loving God is. He became a servant to all, letting love lead him to put on humanity. He gave up everything so that we could know God as he truly is, removing every hindrance and boundary that kept us from him. He gave his very life so that we might know the power of his life in ours. He is the overcomer, and we overcome every trial through fellowship with him.

Remember how God has brought you through hard times.

Gift of Grace

By grace you have been saved through faith,
and that not of yourselves; it is the gift of God.

EPHESIANS 2:8 NKJV

Nothing we achieve in this life can earn us favor in the eyes of God. Though we may be successful in many different spheres, our success cannot save us from loss in life. It cannot avoid the inevitable pitfalls of humanity. Only God can save us fully and wholly. Only his love can truly set us free.

God has gifted us unhindered fellowship with him through his Son, Jesus. There is more than enough grace for all who have ever and will ever live, breathe, and move on this earth. Christ is the living reflection of God's unfailing love. Let's lean into the grace of God in our weakness and rely on his power to help us in our frailty. Where we are stuck in cycles that just won't quit, he is the power that breaks through on our behalf and sets our feet on the steady rock of his love. His grace is free for all, and it is ours through Christ!

Thank God for his grace that continually strengthens and saves you.

Glorious Possibilities

"Things never discovered or heard of before, things beyond our ability to imagine these are the many things God has in store for all his lovers."

1 CORINTHIANS 2:9 TPT

When was the last time you dreamed of something beyond your current reality and just allowed your heart to hope? When our minds are overly focused on the what-ifs and worries of the unknown, anxiety can overtake our systems. But when we learn to ground ourselves in the incomparable goodness, faithfulness, and nearness of God, we can dream with open hearts rather than dread closing us in.

Nothing is impossible for God. He will always be faithful in his Word and to every one of his promises. There are more beautiful things in store than we can imagine. What would it do to our hearts if we stretched our imaginations in God's love? We cannot exaggerate his goodness! We can never reach the limits of his powerful affection.

Submit your mind to Christ. Ask him to stretch your imagination with the possibilities of his goodness.

Called into the Light

You are a chosen people, royal priests, a holy nation, a people for God's own possession. You were chosen to tell about the wonderful acts of God, who called you out of darkness into his wonderful light.

1 PETER 2:9 NCV

In the light of God's presence, nothing is hidden. There are no shadows in his love. He clarifies what was once blurry and unclear. Let us first come into his light today, for he shines brightly on each one of us. Look to him, and you will find that he is already closer than you thought.

As people chosen by God to be sons and daughters, may we never forget the privilege of sharing his unrelenting love with all who will listen. The same love that calls us children beckons to those who have not yet heard its call. May we be generous, kind, and merciful just as God our Father is. Let us shine bright as beacons of hope.

Tell someone today about something wonderful God has done for you.

God's People

Once you were not a people,
but now you are God's people;
once you had not received mercy,
but now you have received mercy.

1 PETER 2:10 ESV

As a child of God, you have unending mercy from the Father's heart. You cannot mess up so bad that he will turn you away when you come to him. His love is evident in the parable of the prodigal son. After the son left his father's home and wasted his inheritance on foolish pursuits, he returned in shame and defeat. What was the father's response? It was to run to meet him as soon as he saw the son walking home! He covered his son with his robes and ordered a celebration for his return.

The Father does not heap punishment on us when we return to him. No, he orders a feast, and he welcomes us back into the comfort of his home. May we never stay away from his heart for fear of his response toward our rebellion.

*As often as you think of it today,
thank God for being your good Father.*

Spirit Strength

We did not receive the spirit of this world system but the Spirit of God, so that we might come to understand and experience all that grace has lavished upon us.

1 CORINTHIANS 2:12 TPT

The spirit of this world leads us in fear and keeps us in limited understanding of the scope of the beauty of life. In the Spirit of God, there is more than enough joy, peace, patience, kindness, hope, and love. This is an every moment, always-available abundance provided for us. Where others seek to keep us in our place, God's love sets us free to run in the open fields of opportunity.

There is so much grace available. God gives us an aggressive amount of mercy. It never, ever ends. His love is bigger than the ever-expanding universe we inhabit. There is no limit to his kindness. It is from the generosity and abundance of his love that we live, move, and have our being. May we run free in the great wide open of his gracious heart.

Lean into the Spirit's help to understand your freedom in Christ.

Signs of Spring

The flowers appear on the earth,
the time of singing has come,
and the voice of the turtledove is heard in our land.

SONG OF SOLOMON 2:12 ESV

After a long winter, we look for signs of spring like we look for hidden treasure. Nature follows the order of the seasons, and we get to partake in the beauty of each one. The darkness and cold of winter do not last forever. It is a season of burrowing in, slowing down, and resting deeply. After winter comes spring. New life comes out of the dormant earth where death was sown.

Whatever kind of winter you have faced, know that spring is on the horizon. The time of singing is coming again. The birds will return, voicing their jubilee. May you find yourself refreshed in the small, simple hope that blooms around you. There is beauty to find, and there is hope for what lies ahead. Newness is coming, and life will be abundant once more.

Focus on small, ordinary joys today.

Faithful and True

If we are not faithful, he will still be faithful,
because he must be true to who he is.

2 TIMOTHY 2:13 NCV

God's faithfulness is not dependent upon our own. How amazing is that? He is faithful and true because that is his very nature, and he cannot go against it. His love leads him to follow through on all of his promises. They are not empty words spoken by a forgetful man. God is loyal to his vows, and he will not forget a single one of them.

Take hope today in the trustworthy devotion of your God to his holy Word. He will not change. He will not let go of you, no matter how far you stray. His love reaches you no matter where you run. If you went to the highest heights, there he would be. If you burrowed into a cave in the middle of the earth, you could not escape him. He is good, he is reliable, and he is merciful. Trust him!

Where are you discouraged by lack of follow-through in your life? Look to God's unfailing faithfulness.

Ever So Near

You have been united with Christ Jesus. Once you were far away from God, but now you have been brought near to him through the blood of Christ.

EPHESIANS 2:13 NLT

God is not housed or confined in a physical temple. He is greater than the universe, and in him all things find their being. God is so much greater than humankind, who are limited by flesh and bones. He is spirit, and he is the source of everything. He moves where he pleases. Like the wind, he rushes in. Like oxygen, he is the atmosphere that gives us life.

The blood of Christ has brought us close to God. It is the power that forever demolished anything that would keep us separated from his love. As his people, he moves freely in us. When we surrender our lives to him, he transforms us by his power. He is ever so near. In our heartbreak and in our greatest joys, he is with us.

Close your eyes, take a deep breath, and thank God for being as close as the air you breathe.

God's Desire

God is working in you, giving you the desire
and the power to do what pleases him.

PHILIPPIANS 2:13 NLT

It is God's work in us that compels and empowers us to do what pleases him. And what is it that pleases God? It is for us to live submitted to his love, filled up on the truth of his mercy and extending it to others. His law of love is simple, and his grace is sufficient to help us.

What desires do you find yourself living to satisfy? In Romans 7, Paul remarked that he kept doing what he didn't want to do. Our weakness can either cause us to lean into the grace and strength of God or lead us to give into what we would not otherwise do in a healthy state. Praise God that we have access to the fellowship of the Spirit who helps us when we cannot choose goodness on our own. Even when we fail, he is the mercy that holds and uplifts us.

*Relate to someone today with empathy,
extending the same love that God offers.*

Fragrant Grace

Thanks be to God, who always leads us as captives in Christ's triumphal procession and uses us to spread the aroma of the knowledge of him everywhere.

2 CORINTHIANS 2:14 NIV

The victory of Christ is our victory. We do not depend on our own feeble attempts at holiness to save ourselves, let alone anyone else. We have been wrapped up, covered, and completely purified in the great love of our God and King. His resurrection power is the power that raises us to life in him.

May we meditate on the overcoming power of Jesus today. The same Spirit that raised him from the grave is the Spirit who dwells with us. We are overcomers by the blood of the Lamb, and there is nothing that can keep us from his mercy. Thanks be to God, who always leads us in the victory of Jesus through this life. What a Savior. What a leader! What a King. No one can undo what he has done.

Share your joy in Christ with someone today.

Perfect Peace

He himself is our peace, who has made us both one and
has broken down in his flesh the dividing wall
of hostility.

EPHESIANS 2:14 ESV

There is no shortage of hostilities in this world. Everywhere we look, dividing lines are all around us, pushing us further from each other and shouting for us to take sides. Jesus does not join this chorus. He does not demand that we ridicule those we do not agree with. In fact, his love requires us to offer understanding and compassion, rather than cold shoulders and apathy.

The love of God is the promotion of peace and unity in Christ. He brings together all things that do not seem to naturally mesh. His kingdom is full of diversity and the beauty of different expressions of his goodness. Let's be quick to humble our hearts in love when judgment rushes to the forefront of our thoughts. The way of Christ is peace, and we are called to be promoters of his loving unity in a world that seeks to divide.

Practice promoting peace in your relationships today.

Our Inheritance

He gave himself for us so he might pay the price to free us from all evil and to make us pure people who belong only to him—people who are always wanting to do good deeds.

TITUS 2:14 NCV

It is almost too much to comprehend that God would give himself to us in Jesus and that he would pave the way for our freedom from the cycles of sin, shame, and death. All he wants is our fellowship; he wants us to know him and to live in the glorious freedom of his love. He knows us better than we know ourselves, leading us with wisdom that is for our good.

The power of Christ's death and resurrection did not end with the early church. It is as applicable today as it ever was or will be. The potency of his mercy is enough to raise the dead to life, to free the captive, and to heal every broken body. Jesus is our great liberator. May we live in the freedom that he has offered us, not letting shame convince us otherwise. It is for freedom that we have been set free (Galatians 1:5).

Thank God for the freedom you have in his love.

Sweet Message

The Messiah has come to preach this sweet message of peace to you, the ones who were distant, and to those who are near.

EPHESIANS 2:17 TPT

The inclusivity of Christ's invitation to peace with God is a beautiful thing. He does not disregard anyone with his love. No one is left out of his affection. His love compels him to advocate for us, to draw us to himself with kindness, and to fight for our freedom. This is as true for those we struggle to get along with as it is for those we adore.

May we never fall into the trap of thinking that Christ's message of peace is only for people we like. Jesus spent his time on this earth ministering to the outcasts of society as often, if not more than, the time he spent with those who already claimed to know and love God. May our hearts be malleable in his love, letting his compassion transform our perceptions of people. What a glorious God that he would call us to himself. We have been offered the generosity of abundant love, so let us love others in the same way.

Offer kindness and prayers for someone you struggle with.

He Knows

He suffered and endured every test and temptation, so that he can help us every time we pass through the ordeals of life.

HEBREWS 2:18 TPT

Jesus is our great High Priest. He is not only God; he is also fully man. He experienced the full spectrum of humanity, and he knows what it is to be weak and to be tempted. He was vulnerable as we all are in our mortal bodies. He experienced hunger, exhaustion, irritation, and grief. Let us not forget that Jesus knows what living on this earth is like. He knows.

Jesus spent forty days in a desert being tempted in all ways that we are tempted, and yet he did not sin. We lean on his strength, given to us through his Spirit. He is our help when we have no power to break through on our own. Jesus advocates for us through endless prayer to the Father. He is the best advocate because he knows our struggle intimately. Let us take comfort in his understanding. Let us rely on his strength to empower us and to guide us through our own temptations.

In your weakness, remember that Jesus experienced the fullness of humanity.

More Than Enough

My old self has been crucified with Christ. It is no longer I who live, but Christ lives in me. So I live in this earthly body by trusting in the Son of God, who loved me and gave himself for me.

GALATIANS 2:20 NLT

When we rely on our own strength to get us to where we want to go, we will only get so far. Our resources are not endless, and we will find that something has to give along the way. The good mews of Christ isn't simply that someday we will be saved from the pain and suffering of this world and welcomed into his kingdom that will never end, though that is good news. The good news is that Christ is with us now.

Through his Spirit, Christ lives in us, giving us access to the endless resources of his kingdom love. Our lives have been made new in him, and we do not live for the satisfaction of our simple and fleshly desires. There is purpose, there is openness and space, and there is freedom in him. Let's continue to trust the Lord to lead us into his goodness.

Honor Jesus by remembering him with your choices today.

March

Devote yourselves to prayer
with an alert mind
and a thankful heart.

COLOSSIANS 4:2 NLT

Revealer of Mysteries

"He reveals deep and secret things;
He knows what is in the darkness,
and light dwells with Him."

DANIEL 2:22 NKJV

There is nothing in this world, or outside of it, that is a mystery to God. He sees the creatures of the deep seas, which we are still discovering. He knows the number of grains of sand on every beach, and he understands the workings of every organism. In the far reaches of the universe, he can be found in fullness. In the space where you are right now, there he is, too.

When worry about the unknowns of the future have you restless and circling, God's faithfulness is unchanged. He sees what is in the darkness as well as in the light. He knows every possible outcome for each and every situation. Turn to him with your anxious thoughts and yield your heart to him. He is faithful, he is true, and nothing surprises him. Trust him, for he is the same God who delivered you before. He will do it again, and he will give you peace in the process.

Give God your worries and rest in his faithfulness.

Refreshing Rains

Rejoice, you people of Jerusalem! Rejoice in the LORD
your God! For the rain he sends demonstrates his
faithfulness. Once more the autumn rains will come, as
well as the rains of spring.

JOEL 2:23 NLT

After a drought, rain is a cause for celebration. After a long
winter, the melting of snow and the budding of new life
is reason to rejoice. Even in the mess of muddy puddles,
there is joy and hope. The transition from one season to
the next is often messy, but there is so much beauty in this
passage of time.

Where you look and see puddles in your life, know that this
is a sign of God's refreshing waters pooling. There is new
life coming, and though it may look messy at the moment,
it is the necessary awkwardness between seasons. His
faithfulness comes like the rains of springtime. Surely there
is good ahead, and the seeds that were sown in barrenness
will break through the ground with vigor.

*Note where you see the rains of God's faithfulness
in your life today.*

Hope for Tomorrow

The threshing floors will again be piled high with grain,
and the presses will overflow with new wine and olive oil.

JOEL 2:24 NLT

Sometimes, in order to look ahead with hope, we must look behind to remember the faithfulness of God where we have already experienced it. Have you known safety and security in your home life or in relationships? Have you ever gotten out of a terrible situation and lived to talk about it? Look back over your history and ask God to reveal to you where he was and what he was doing.

As you remember the pockets of goodness in your life, may you also find that hope springs up for the possibilities that lie ahead of you. Where there have been promises fulfilled in your life, there are still some that you are waiting on. Take courage today, knowing that the God who hung the stars in the heavens is the God who follows through on his promises. He will not fail you. There is life and hope ahead.

Remember the promises that God has spoken over you.

Trustworthy Truth

His anointing teaches you about everything, and is true, and is no lie—just as it has taught you, abide in him.

1 JOHN 2:27 ESV

Jesus is the way, the truth, and the life. He is wisdom personified. He is merciful, and he is powerful to save. May you find yourself wrapped tightly to his heart of love today. May it be your source, your strength, and your guiding light. There is no shadow in Christ, for he is the Light of the world.

Let us turn every question and every problem over to him who lights up the darkest night. He shines brighter than the sun, and his wisdom brings clarity to our confusion. We can trust that what he says is true. His Word is reliable, and his promises are sure. When we align ourselves in his love and choose to follow him in humble submission, we will find that the truth sets us free.

Mindfully choose God's ways
over your own preferences today.

Greater Things

"I will pour out my spirit on all flesh; your sons and your daughters shall prophesy, your old men shall dream dreams, and your young men shall see visions."

JOEL 2:28 NRSV

If our faith does not lead us into real and living relationship with the Father of love, then we are not experiencing the fullness of what Christ offers us. It was prophesied that the Spirit of God would be poured out on all, some prophesying of what is to come, others dreaming meaningful dreams, and still others seeing visions of God's glory.

When Jesus was getting ready to return to heaven, he told his disciples that they, and all who would follow him, would do even greater miracles than he did in his ministry. This is through the power of the Spirit of God, poured out on us through relationship with Christ. The power of God is the seal of his presence. He moves through the natural in seemingly impossible ways. Are we living with his power made evident in our lives?

Ask the Holy Spirit to broaden your understanding of his power.

Children of God

See what kind of love the Father has given to us,
that we should be called children of God; and so we are.
The reason why the world does not know us is that it
did not know him.

1 JOHN 3:1 ESV

As children of God, we can come boldly before his throne
at any time, knowing we will be met by his love. Whenever
we call on him, we have his attention. He is not distracted,
and he is not too busy for us. He is not limited in time or
awareness. He is always mindful of us, never forgetting
what we need or failing to show up in present mercy.

May we live with the confidence of dearly loved sons and
daughters. Though others may not be able to understand
us, we have a good father who always does. We live for his
kingdom come and his will being done on the earth, not
for our own bellies or pockets. May we continue to turn
continually to our Father in both our time of need and in
times of rest.

*Soak in the reality of your identity as a child of God
and what that means.*

Even When

The Lord Yahweh is always faithful to place you on a firm foundation and guard you from the Evil One.

2 Thessalonians 3:3 TPT

No matter how many times we falter in life, God's faithfulness will never run out. His loyalty is not dependent upon our own. Even when we doubt, God's truth stands firm. Even when we cannot make sense of our situations, God's wisdom is unmoved. Even when we run away from him, God's love is reaching after us in the same, unending measure.

We rely on our God to put us on the firm foundation of his faithfulness. We depend on him to keep us there. With hearts of submission, when we trust the Lord to do what we cannot, hope keeps us tethered to him. His strong love will never let us go, even when we struggle to recognize how it holds us. May we weave our hope around the faithfulness of our God, keeping our eyes on him.

Put your hope in God's faithfulness rather than your own ability.

Empowered

We don't see ourselves as capable enough to do anything in our own strength, for our true competence flows from God's empowering presence.

2 CORINTHIANS 3:5 TPT

God's grace is the force that empowers us to live with love as our banner. More than a motivation, it becomes the air we breathe. We breathe in the power of God's mercy, and we let it out as we live out his love in practical ways. Thankfully, we do not have to depend on our own reserves of waning strength to do any of it.

Right here and now, there is an abundance of grace and strength in the presence of the Lord. There is more than enough power to help us overcome our fears. There is space to take the time to heal and to extend that same grace to others. God's empowering presence fills and flows from us, releasing the fruit of his Spirit into our hearts, our homes, and our lives.

Focus on what you already have instead of what you lack today.

Led by Mercy

May the Lord lead your hearts into a full understanding
and expression of the love of God and the patient
endurance that comes from Christ.

2 Thessalonians 3:5 NLT

It is not possible to expand our minds to fully understand
God's love. Though we may try to comprehend with our
own capabilities, it is the Spirit who leads us into revelation
and knowledge of his great and expansive compassion.
God, in his kindness, draws us further into the depths of his
mercy and increases our capacity to grasp his goodness.

In the vastness of God's heart, we find that patience is
easier to practice. Endurance is more readily available to
us through the strength of his presence with us. There
is more than enough to get us through every trial and
trouble. Every hard conversation, every trauma, and every
unexpected problem is a place of opportunity to root
ourselves the present peace of God who carries us through
every moment.

Practice patience as you go throughout your day.

Washed and Renewed

He saved us, not on the basis of deeds
which we have done in righteousness,
but according to His mercy,
by the washing of regeneration
and renewing by the Holy Spirit.

TITUS 3:5 NASB

There is no shortage of ideals in this world. Though we may love our lives, if we spend too much time looking at what others have, we may lose sight of how blessed we already are. In an age where social media presents highlight reels as reality, we must fight against the urge of competitive comparison.

In Christ, we are all on the same playing field. There is no hierarchy in his kingdom. We are brothers and sisters, not masters and servants. May we resist the false narrative that our choices make us better than others who choose differently. The inheritance of his kingdom is the same for each one of us as his children. May we be free to live in the renewal that he offers us through his Spirit, and not bound to strive after unsatisfying goals.

Recognize where comparison has kept you from being yourself and choose differently today.

In All Things

Seek his will in all you do,
and he will show you which path to take.

PROVERBS 3:6 NLT

Whether or not we take him up on his offer, God is always willing and ready to lead us in his love. He counsels us in his wisdom, and he guides us in the truth of his mercy. Not every decision we make will be cut and dry, but the freedom to choose in line with his kingdom values will help us.

When we look to the fruit of the Holy Spirit, we see the evidence of what God's nature is like, and we learn how he moves. Where there is profound peace, God is with us. Where there is loving acceptance, he is there. Where there is patience, kindness, joy, and self-control, the Spirit is behind it. Let us not simply look to the rules of how to live. Instead, let us look for the nature of our good God in the paths we choose.

*Look for God's wisdom to guide you
as you make decisions today.*

Joy in Fellowship

How can we thank God enough for you
in return for all the joy we have
in the presence of our God because of you?

1 THESSALONIANS 3:9 NIV

There is tremendous healing in the company of those who bring us deep joy. When we know the fellowship of loyal friends, how could we but give thanks to God for them? It is a gift to be seen, known, and supported. Acceptance and belonging are what we long for, and when we find it in a group of people, there is reason to rejoice!

We were not created to be islands, living parallel but disconnected lives. We were made for community, our lives interwoven in a tapestry of grace. May we not forget the significance of meeting together with those we trust. May we open our hearts toward one another in love instead of pushing each other away in fear. There is so much joy in fellowship with kingdom-minded people.

Call someone who gives you joy and let them know how much they mean to you.

Grounded in Goodness

The Lord is not slow in doing what he promised—
the way some people understand slowness.
But God is being patient with you.
He does not want anyone to be lost,
but he wants all people to change their hearts and lives.

2 PETER 3:9 NCV

God's timing is his own. He does not need our platitudes or our reasoning to be convinced of why he should move quicker than he does. He does not need us to explain why he should slow down, either. Yet, he is always gracious with us. He hears our honest words, our pleas, and our longings. He does not ignore them.

The Lord is gracious in all that he does. He is patient in love, wanting everyone to experience the transformative power of his mercy. He longs for every living heart to know him as he is, in Spirit and in truth. May our own longings wrap around his so that we become more like him. May we look for opportunities to extend grace, mercy, kindness, peace, and joy to others.

Take an opportunity to empathize with someone today.

Just a Glimpse

God has made everything beautiful for its own time.
He has planted eternity in the human heart,
but even so, people cannot see the whole scope
of God's work from beginning to end.

ECCLESIASTES 3:11 NLT

Have you ever been so enraptured by the melody of a song or the striking beauty of a sunset that you had no words to describe what you felt? This awe that overcame you is but a glimpse of the glory of God. He is brilliantly beautiful and so much greater than any mind can imagine.

Even so, the beauty we find around us in nature, in people, and in various forms of art are small reflections of the magnificence that we will one day behold when we stand face to face with Jesus. Though we cannot comprehend the vast glory of God's kingdom, we get previews in the ordinary joys of life. May we be people who look for beauty, even in dirt and ashes.

Look for the beauty around you.

Living Love

May the Lord make your love for one another
and for all people grow and overflow.

1 THESSALONIANS 3:12 NLT

There is nothing more important, nothing more sacred, than to live out our love for all to see. Where there is compassion, there is the Spirit of God in our midst. Where mercy moves us, there is where God is leading. Love stretches us beyond the boundaries that would have us stay small and safe. It takes us to places we may have never chosen on our own. Love leads us in life, always.

When we look at our lives, where do we see the marks of God's mercy? Where does love ring loudest? May we never grow stagnant in apathy, for that is the opposite of God's mercy. Let's fill up every day on his new mercies that refresh, renew, restore, and refuel us to keep pressing on and pressing in with love to those around us.

*Reach out in love beyond the boundaries
of your little life today.*

Clothed in Compassion

Put on then, as God's chosen ones,
holy and beloved, compassionate hearts,
kindness, humility, meekness, and patience.

COLOSSIANS 3:12 ESV

What marks us as people of God is not our doctrine, how we dress, or what we say. It's how we live. More aptly, it's how we love. When we clothe ourselves with compassion, keeping our hearts open to love, we reflect the heart of our good Father. When we move with kindness, we reveal the kindness of Jesus.

With humble hearts that are not too proud to admit when we were wrong or did not know the full story, we reflect the humble nature of Christ, who, though he was God, lived as a modest man. When we choose meekness, we need not shout our opinions at each other, showing how God does not manipulate or seek to control us. When we live with patience, we reflect the patience of God that wants all to know him.

*Choose compassion where you would rather
turn a cold shoulder today.*

Confident and Free

In him and through faith in him we may approach God with freedom and confidence.

EPHESIANS 3:12 NIV

What God does not hold against us, may we never hold against ourselves. We have been set free in the great power of Christ, who rose from the dead after he was crucified and buried. He resurrected to life, and by that same power, we come alive in him. There is now nothing that keeps us from his overwhelming affection.

May we approach God with confidence, knowing that we are met with mercy every time we turn to him. Kindness overflows from his heart. There is an abundance of grace to strengthen us in our frailty. There is freedom from our addictions, our shame, and our fears. There is nothing that can stand against the power of our God. Let us run to him in the liberty that is already ours in Christ. Let's run straight into the open arms of our Father.

Thank God for the freedom you have in Christ.

Leave Room

Make allowance for each other's faults,
and forgive anyone who offends you.
Remember, the Lord forgave you,
so you must forgive others.

COLOSSIANS 3:13 NLT

When we live with the expectation of God's goodness meeting us every day, we will find that there are opportunities everywhere to choose his ways over our own. His goodness meets us in the softening of our hearts in his compassion. It meets us in deep laughter with friends. It meets us in the camaraderie of a shared experience.

Do we leave room for other people's faults? None of us is perfect in love, and we will hurt each other along the way. When we keep offense from our hearts, choosing to forgive instead of holding onto bitterness, we exhibit the same kind of mercy we receive in God's love. We have been forgiven for our faults, so let us also forgive the faults of others. God is full of mercy, and he is also just. We can trust him in all things.

Give the benefit of the doubt to someone you have been struggling to understand.

Confident Expectation

I don't depend on my own strength to accomplish this; however I do have one compelling focus: I forget all of the past as I fasten my heart to the future instead.

PHILIPPIANS 3:13 TPT

Our lives are made up of little choices, multiple small movements, and intentions. We have built up to where we stand right in this moment. Though we cannot predict the unknown challenges or trials that will arise and shift our course, we can know this: God is with us through it all. He faithfully guides us through the darkest nights, just as certainly as he does on our clearest days.

When we overly depend on our own abilities to thrive, we will be disappointed. We are not infinite in resources. But God is! His grace and mercy are always available to us, whenever we need it, in abundance. May we look to the future with hope, knowing that the one who guides us is the one who is with us. He has gone before us, and he is sowing seeds of his goodness into the path we walk.

*Be mindful of choosing to trust God
in the little things today.*

Always

May the Lord of peace himself give you peace
at all times in every way.

2 Thessalonians 3:16 esv

God is endlessly good. He does not put stipulations on his
peace, and he doesn't put parameters on his love. They are
so much greater than we, in our humanity, can imagine. He
soothes the worries of our hearts with his present peace
when we turn to him. He unfurls the crinkles on our brows
with the tender touch of his presence.

No matter where this finds you today, know that God is
overflowing with love, peace, and joy over you today. Invite
his presence to flood your mind, your heart, and your
body with the calming rays of his love. In him, you will find
profound peace. He is as confident and true as he has ever
been, no matter what you are feeling. Turn to him with an
open heart and let him love you to life again.

Seek God's peace in turning your heart to him in every
worry and anxiety. Thank him for his presence.

As Long as I Live

Every Scripture has been written by the Holy Spirit, the breath of God. It will empower you by its instruction and correction, giving you the strength to take the right direction and lead you deeper into the path of godliness.

2 TIMOTHY 3:16 TPT

In the Word, there is a wealth of wisdom to instruct us in God's kingdom ways. His Word is clear that his ways are higher than our own. His ways are better than the ways of humankind. Where we are quick to anger, he is patient in love. Where we are prone to judgment, he extends mercy. Where we put restrictions in place to control outcomes, he frees us from the expectations of others and gives us liberty to transform.

There will never come a day when God's Word is not relevant to our lives. Though our understanding will transform along with revelation and deepening relationship with the Lord, his truth remains the same simple and powerful truth. May we look to him and find the strength we need to follow after him.

Take time to meditate on God's Word today, receiving the gift of accessing his wisdom.

Higher Wisdom

Let the word of Christ dwell in you richly, teaching and admonishing one another in all wisdom, singing Psalms and hymns and spiritual songs, with thankfulness in your hearts to God.

COLOSSIANS 3:16 ESV

When our hearts overflow with thanksgiving, it will spill over into our how we express ourselves throughout the day. Have you ever woken up with a song running through your head? Have you ever found yourself so happy that you had to sing about it? Singing to the Lord is one of the sweetest exchanges you can make. Melodies and harmonies move us in ways that simple speech cannot.

When we fill our hearts and minds with the Word of God, meditating on the love of Christ, our hearts will build up with his truth. When we submit to wisdom, we can encourage one another in it. When we sing our praise to God, filling our consciousness with gratitude, we connect to the eternal goodness of his being. May we lift our hearts, songs, and lives to him!

Sing your thanks to God today!

Lavish Liberty

The Lord is the Spirit,
and wherever the Spirit of the Lord is,
there is freedom.

2 Corinthians 3:17 NLT

There is nowhere that the Spirit is not. With that in mind, the statement "wherever the Spirit of the Lord is, there is freedom" resounds loudly with hope. God himself is the Spirit, and he is not bound by space, time, or matter. He moves freely, and he is full of liberation from everything that keeps us stuck.

Wherever you are today, the Spirit of the Lord is with you, and if the Spirit of the Lord is with you, there is freedom for you. Where fear tries to hem you in and keep you small, the Lord's love sets you free to grow, explore, and expand. Look at the areas where you feel trapped. Consider that there is an invitation for greater liberty in the love of God today. Submit your heart, your thoughts, and your life to the Lord, and he will lead you in the deliverance from every one of your fears.

Choose freedom over fear today.

Purpose

Whatever you do in word or deed,
do all in the name of the Lord Jesus,
giving thanks through Him to God the Father.

COLOSSIANS 3:17 NASB

Nothing we do in this life, no matter how small it seems, is meaningless. We can know the profound purpose of God in even the most menial of tasks. Our mindset will either lend to this sense of purpose or distract us from it. It is important that we know that every moment is a choice, and every choice is ours to make.

Whatever we do, when we do it for the Lord, it is a fragrant offering to him. May we take the time to connect to God through his Spirit's presence today. If we have forgotten the purpose that he has put in us, let's ask him for a reminder of what truly matters. His requirements are simple, yet their impact resounds into eternity. With eyes fixed on Jesus and hearts open to his leading, we will know the deep joy of abiding in him as we move about our normal routines.

Thank God for the purpose you have in him.

Not on You

"God did not send his Son into the world to judge the world guilty, but to save the world through him."

JOHN 3:17 NCV

What is the level of guilt or shame that you deal with on a normal basis? Is it an endless cycle that you cannot seem to escape? Have you begun to believe that it is simply a part of the human struggle? Jesus came to set you free from the cycles of shame, guilt, and fear that keep you from freely moving in his love.

When you turn to the Lord, is there hesitation in your heart? Do you expect his disapproval and his disappointment? This is not how your good Father welcomes you. He has done everything necessary to break down the walls that keep you from living in the abundance of his mercy. He is full of love toward you; even his correction is done with kindness. May you come to him today, laying down your defenses and letting him speak his truth over your identity. Your salvation is dependent on him, not on you.

Let go of the judgment you have carried toward yourself and thank God for his endless mercy.

Never Alone

The LORD your God is in your midst,
a mighty one who will save;
he will rejoice over you with gladness;
he will quiet you by his love;
he will exult over you with loud singing.

ZEPHANIAH 3:17 ESV

The Lord's love is not passive. It is not timid or hesitant. It does not stay away for fear of rejection. It does not pretend to not care. It does not self-protect, it is not harsh or critical, and it is not anxious. It does not avoid harsh realities or hard questions. It is not afraid to show passion, and it is not concerned about how it might be perceived or misrepresented.

The love of the Lord is constantly covering us, chasing us down, lifting our burdens, washing away the dust of our regret, and renewing our hope. However lonely we feel, however overcome by helplessness, the love of the Lord is our constant companion. How could this be? The Lord is the Spirit, and the Spirit of the Lord is with those who yield their lives to him. God is love, and love is with us.

Write a thank you note to the Lord for a specific instance where he has helped you.

Transformed

We all, with unveiled face, beholding the glory of the
Lord, are being transformed into the same image from
one degree of glory to another. For this comes from the
Lord who is the Spirit.

2 CORINTHIANS 3:18 ESV

The most efficient way to transform our lives is to mindfully
choose where our attention goes. Those we spend time
with will affect how we act. What we spend time listening
to and watching will influence our thinking. Where we put
our mental energy will drive the choices we make.

When we give our attention to Jesus, spending time in
prayer and in his Word, we will become more like him.
As we behold the beauty of God in worship, considering
the glory of his unmatched nature, we are filled with the
wonder of his goodness. As this wonder works its way
through our systems, our thoughts transform in the great
expanse of his presence. May we be people who take
autonomy over our choices, for they are powerful agents
of transformation and change. As we choose to look to the
Lord, we will find more freedom than we can now imagine.

Be mindful of your choices today.

Even Greater Than

This is how we know that we belong to the truth
and how we set our hearts at rest in his presence:
If our hearts condemn us, we know that God is greater
than our hearts, and he knows everything.

1 John 3:19 NIV

One of the most beautiful experiences we can have with
the Lord is the relief we find in his presence. He does not
hold our sins against us, and he doesn't look for perfection
from us. He doesn't have unrealistic standards that are
out of reach. Where we are continually missing the mark,
he has already met and satisfied it. May we know the
deep rest, acceptance, and liberation of his love that has
provided all that we need.

Even if we find that our hearts continually condemn us,
struggling to grasp this liberating reality, we know that
God is greater than our hearts. He knows everything. He is
better than our hearts. His wisdom is full of truth, and his
truth trumps our understanding. May we dare to believe
that God is as good as his love. He is infinitely better
than we could ever imagine. We cannot exaggerate his
goodness!

Recognize that God is better than you
and thank him for his love toward you.

Small but Sure

The Sovereign LORD is my strength!
He makes me as surefooted as a deer,
able to tread upon the heights.

HABAKKUK 3:19 NLT

In the freedom of God's love, he guides us. We get to choose how we will live, and the voice of wisdom leads us as we venture along. How unmatched his understanding is! He is not afraid of our mess-ups or our blatant defiance to obedience. We are like children testing the waters of independence. His love is strong enough to hold us even when we make mistakes.

When we rely on the Lord as our strength, he builds our confidence in his ability to lead us. He is always faithful, and he is always able to direct us on the paths of his peace. Every moment is an opportunity to lean into his grace. As we follow after him, growing stronger in conviction of his faithfulness, we are able to walk on even the rockiest of trails without slipping, for he is our guide and companion.

Let God lead you in small and big ways today.

Weak Ones

"Behold, at that time I will deal with all your oppressors.
And I will save the lame and gather the outcast,
and I will change their shame into praise
and renown in all the earth."

ZEPHANIAH 3:19 ESV

The Lord is mindful of us in our weakness. He sees the vulnerable, and he cares for them more than we could ever imagine doing in our own compassion. He gathers those that the world casts out. He does not deny a place in his kingdom to anyone who looks to him for help and for hope.

When we look at the life of Jesus, we see this kind of love on display. He touched lepers and healed their contagious disease! These people were shunned by society. He advocated for women, breaking the norms of the culture. He ate with tax collectors who were hated by their peers. He is the God who goes to the margins. May we reflect his love by doing the same.

Thank Jesus for the faithfulness of his love.

True Home

Our homeland is in heaven, and we are waiting for our
Savior, the Lord Jesus Christ, to come from heaven.

PHILIPPIANS 3:20 NCV

It is important that we not lose sight of where our true
home is. We are like wanderers in the desert of this world,
waiting to enter the promised land of God's great kingdom.
Though we experience glimpses of the glory that awaits us,
the promise of the pure goodness of his eternal kingdom
keeps us pressing in and pressing on in hard times.

May we be aware of what we are building with our lives.
Are we building a kingdom with our comfort in mind,
or are we building on the foundation of God's kingdom,
knowing that the greatest treasures are yet to come?
When disappointment in this world, its systems, and the
brokenness of humanity is overwhelming, may we redirect
our attention to Jesus Christ. He is the King of kings and
the Lord of lords, and he will make all wrong things right.
Let's look to him and to his kingdom that is coming.

Remember the hope of heaven
when discouragement sets in.

April

Praise the LORD.
Give thanks to the LORD,
for he is good;
his love endures forever.

PSALM 106:1 NIV

Called Out

"Listen! I am standing at the door, knocking;
if you hear my voice and open the door,
I will come in to you and eat with you,
and you with me."

REVELATION 3:20 NRSV

Jesus is standing at the door of our hearts, knocking. When we hear his voice and open the door, he comes in and makes himself at home. It is never too late to answer the call of his beckoning. He does not grow weary, and he never tires. He is forever our advocate, our faithful friend, and the truth that sets us free.

Today, wherever this finds you, may you take the opportunity to listen for the Lord and to welcome his fellowship in your life. He is not silent. He has not left you or turned away. His companionship will bring you life and meaning. His instruction will bring you freedom and peace. Lean into him, learning the tone of his voice, as well as the nature of his person. He is so very good, and he is near.

Spend time in fellowship with the Lord today.

So Much More

With God's power working in us, God can do much, much more than anything we can ask or imagine.

EPHESIANS 3:21 NCV

Though there is much that we can accomplish on our own when we put grit and determination to it, there is far more that God can do! Let this be an invitation, not to give up our work ethic, but to trust that God will take our little or our much, and he will do even greater things through his resurrection power at work in our lives.

We could never exhaust God's strength. Even if every moment of every day we called upon his name for help, it is but a whisper in the resounding chorus of his faithfulness. May we become audacious in our prayers, asking more boldly, dreaming more wildly of what he can accomplish. And more than that, let us lean into his nature, knowing him more and more. As we do, our faith will grow.

Thank God for his power at work in your life.

Heart and Soul

Put your heart and soul into every activity you do,
as though you are doing it for the Lord himself
and not merely for others.

COLOSSIANS 3:23 TPT

If we wait around for motivation to get going, excuses
are plentiful. We could continue to put off until later what
we could do quite easily right now. We don't need to feel
inspired in order to choose to be consistent. When we
realize the power of our choices, we take ownership over
each one, whether or not it falls in line with our goals.

May we choose with intention today rather than making
excuses for our self-sabotage. Let us commit everything
we do to the Lord who sees it all and will not forget. When
we align our lives in the love of God, we pattern them after
his kingdom principles. There is room to choose rest, to
choose joy, to choose peace. There is also room to choose
compassion that moves us out of our comfort zones,
to move a step closer to our goals, to choose kindness
instead of judgment. May we make choices that line up
with Jesus' ways.

Commit your daily activities to God today.

Plentiful Hope

"The Lord is my portion," says my soul,
"therefore I will hope in him."

LAMENTATIONS 3:24 ESV

When hope is in deficit, what do you do? Where do you turn? It is not a sin to experience low moments in life. It is not a betrayal to your faith to question your previously held beliefs. Jesus is the way, the truth, and the life. Yet there are many things wrapped around our belief systems that are not based in him, but rather based in cultural, familial, and societal conditioning.

Our understanding is not full. We see through a glass darkly, as Paul put it in 1 Corinthians. We know in part, but when we are face to face with the Lord Jesus, we will know fully. May we look to Jesus first, may we look to him most, and may we measure all of our beliefs by his Word, his nature, and his love. He is our abundant portion of peace, of joy, and of hope.

Put your hope in who Jesus was, is, and always will be.

No Reason to Fear

When you lie down, you will not be afraid;
when you lie down, your sleep will be sweet.

PROVERBS 3:24 NIV

When worries overtake our minds, sending anxiety signals to our nervous systems, we can receive the peace of God to calm the chaos. His peace is plentiful in every moment, and it is sufficient to calm, comfort, and soothe us. We do not need to entertain the swirling thoughts that play out unknown situations. We can find relief in the very present nearness of our God.

Practice putting your trust in God's faithfulness by turning your attention to the present moment when worries start to take over your thoughts. Slow down, focusing on the air that you are breathing, noticing the way that it enters and leaves your body. In that space, God is present. Invite his peace as you breathe deeply and release the worries as you let it out. He is near, he is good, and he will take care of you.

*When you lay in your bed tonight,
thank God for his peace.*

Confident Trust

God is your confidence in times of crisis,
keeping your heart at rest in every situation.

PROVERBS 3:26 TPT

In crisis, we are not left alone to scramble in our fight or flight responses. God is our Good Shepherd, he is our defender, and he is our strong and mighty tower of refuge. He is the safe place that we run to. Our souls always have access to his peace. Our spirits know the fellowship of his overpowering love. Let's not forget that the one who has been faithful to his Word will continue to be until every promise he made is fulfilled. And even then, he will continue in loyal love.

Thank God that our confidence is not in ourselves! It is in his reliable nature and resurrection power. It is in him. May we find rest in our hearts as we keep the anchor of our hope tethered to his constant character. He will never change, and we can rely on his strength in every crisis.

*Declare the faithfulness of God
over your current circumstances.*

Healing Is Coming

For you who fear my name,
the sun of righteousness shall rise
with healing in its wings.

MALACHI 4:2 ESV

Our God is powerful to save, to heal, and to restore. His faithfulness is not reserved for the strong. His power is not confined to churches, to temples, or to anything. God's character is full of mercy, full of joy, full of peace, full of goodness. His nature is compassionate, and he is moved in love to meet those who call out to him.

Do we cry out to God for more of him, or do we restrain ourselves? May we never grow tired of asking him for healing, for he loves to express his goodness to us through restoration. There is no heart too broken, no soul too shattered, and no body too weak for him to heal. May we let our hope mingle with his love, knowing that he cares for us. Even in our waiting, may we learn to receive the breakthrough of his power in other areas of life. And let's not give up, for he is good, and he is faithful.

Pray for the healing of a loved one,
knowing God is powerful to do it.

Love that Overcomes

You, dear children, are from God and have overcome
them, because the one who is in you is greater
than the one who is in the world.

1 John 4:4 niv

Jesus is the cornerstone of our faith. Through him,
everything is made clear. He is the wisdom of God
personified. He is the living expression of love. He is the
Savior of all. He is the foundation we build our lives upon,
and he cannot be shaken. He will not be moved! Though
the winds of testing come, when our faith is built upon the
rock of Jesus, we will not be tossed about.

May we take the time to consciously align the values of our
lives with the truth of Jesus Christ. He came to show us the
way to the Father. He revealed the merciful nature of the
Father. He is the way we can approach the throne of heaven
with confidence. He is our covering, he is our mediator, and
he is our stamp of approval before the Father. Let us submit
our minds, our hearts, and our lives to him.

Thank God for the power of Christ's love in your life.

Accept with Thanksgiving

Everything God made is good,
and nothing should be refused
if it is accepted with thanks.

1 TIMOTHY 4:4 NCV

The kingdom of God is not a matter of how we dress, where we worship, what we eat, or our political affiliations. It is not measured by what we restrict. It is not measured by what we allow. There is so much grace and freedom in the love of God. It is not a matter of strict rules over every area of our lives. May we remember this today, and may we practice receiving with thanksgiving what is offered to us.

Let's throw off the guise of perfection as godly and instead let the liberty of God's mercy lead us in gratitude. Kingdom values do not take on specific forms in our diets, our clothing choices, or where we choose to shop. Let's remember that in our freedom, we get to choose how we will live. With gratitude, let's leave the fear of getting it wrong behind and embrace the opportunities to grow, connect, and live with humble hearts.

Receive the gifts today offers you with thanksgiving.

Share in Joy

Rejoice in the Lord always.
I will say it again: Rejoice!

PHILIPPIANS 4:4 NIV

In the presence of God, there is a deep, abiding joy.
Even on our hardest days, his joy is an ever-flowing
undercurrent. As we look for the gifts of God's goodness
in our lives, we will find gratitude fills our hearts when we
discover where he is with us, even in the midst of our pain
and suffering.

No matter what we face, God is with us. His fingerprints of
mercy are all over our lives. When it's hard to see, let's lean
into him and ask for his perspective. He will show us when
we ask him. Moses asked God to reveal his glory, and God
responded. May we never hold back our requests for fear
of rejection. Our God is an all-consuming fire that does not
destroy us but covers us. If there is any reason to rejoice, it
is due to God's presence in our lives. Let us rejoice in him.

Focus on the joys in your life
and let praise to God overflow!

Inherent Worth

Because you are his sons, God sent the Spirit of his Son into our hearts, the Spirit who calls out, "Abba, Father."

GALATIANS 4:6 NIV

As children of the Most High, we find our identity in who God says we are. No matter how inadequate you have felt in life, know that God's Word over you is more powerful. Who he says you are is your true identity. You do not have to live with complete confidence for this to be true. It is dependent on him.

Will you come into agreement with what God says about you? He does not condemn you, he is not apathetic about your life, and he does not wonder whether his power is enough to transform you. Let his love cover you, bringing life to the hopes of your heart, letting the doubts about your goodness go. God created you in his image, and he called you as his own beloved child. You are loved. You are so completely adored! You cannot imagine how deeply and completely he loves you, but give it a try.

Give God your insecurities and thank him
for his acceptance of you.

Love with Intention

Dear friends, let us continue to love one another,
for love comes from God. Anyone who loves
is a child of God and knows God.

1 JOHN 4:7 NLT

The godliest thing we can do in life is to choose to love others as God loves us. This is the kind of love that doesn't give up when things get hard. This love doesn't wait for someone else to make the first move. This love doesn't require reciprocation in order to be shown fully. The love of God is unmetered, unmeasured, and always reaching toward others in overflow.

It is not enough to love someone until we are disappointed by them. Love is a continual choice, a conscious action, and a movement from the fullness of God's love within us. Jesus paved the way to the Father with continual acts of surrender and love. The way we come to God is the same. As we choose to extend mercy to others, we become more and more like God, and we will know him in deeper ways in our relationships.

Spend time with a loved one in a meaningful
and connected way.

Even More Able

We now have this light shining in our hearts, but we ourselves are like fragile clay jars containing this great treasure. This makes it clear that our great power is from God, not from ourselves.

2 CORINTHIANS 4:7 NLT

If we have any encouragement in our frailty, may it be that God is our strength that never runs out. His power is made even more evident in our weakness. When we rely on his grace to empower us to love when we would rather throw stones, it is his nature that shines through.

No matter how much we struggle to choose kindness rather than judgment, we reflect the power of God's love when we do. Even in this, we are not dependent on our own stores of compassion. With hearts connected to God through the Spirit who dwells with us, we receive from his unending mercy. As we are filled with his love, we can give out of his source, overflowing from our hearts to others.

Choose kindness today where your first reaction may be irritation.

Image Bearer

You are no longer a slave, but God's child;
and since you are his child,
God has made you also an heir.

GALATIANS 4:7 NIV

What does it mean to be an image bearer of the Father? How do we show that we belong to him? It is through the generosity of compassion, is it not? When we choose to extend kindness to others, without finding excuses to withhold it, we reflect the mercy of our good Father.

We are not slaves to God. We are not distant relatives, either. We are sons and daughters, children of the Living God. He is generous with all he has. He gives us more than enough grace, love that is constantly overflowing, and access to the deep wells of his joy. His peace is beyond comprehension. His heart is always open. May we generously give to others, moving in the outflow of mercy in our lives and not hoarding it for ourselves. God's kingdom is ever-expanding. Instead of building walls, he invites the nations to himself. May we live with love expanding our borders, as well.

Show generosity today.

Even So

*We are hard pressed on every side, but not crushed;
perplexed, but not in despair.*

2 CORINTHIANS 4:8 NIV

No matter how dark the night gets, there is light somewhere. It is like being in a dark room, thinking that the world has turned black. The rays of the sun are always shining, even in the dead of night when all we can see is its reflection in the moon and stars.

In times of upheaval and disturbing troubles, there is an invitation for us to see beyond our present circumstances. In trials, may we remember that they are passing and will not last. Though we may be pressed on every side, as Paul described, we are not crushed, and we will not be destroyed. Though we may be confused as to what is happening and why, despair is not the answer. Our great God is unmoved in love, in power, and in wisdom. He will come through, and we will see the light of day again.

Look for rays of hope in your day.

Excellent Thoughts

Whatever is true, whatever is honorable, whatever is just, whatever is pure, whatever is pleasing, whatever is commendable, if there is any excellence and if there is anything worthy of praise, think about these things.

PHILIPPIANS 4:8 ESV

Paul did not leave much to mystery when he laid out what godly thinking looks like. The truth of God's Word is simple, not complicated. May we be encouraged with the simplicity of Christ's kingdom values as we take our thoughts captive and turn our attention to what pleases Jesus.

Not all thoughts originate from us. Some are suggestions that we may have overheard. Others may be quotes that people have said. Some will be downright lies. Others will be filled with the truth of God's love. When we have a standard to hold our thoughts up against, it is easier to sift lies from truth. Our biases have no basis in this. Let us use Paul's suggestions as a starting place to regulate our thoughts today.

*Stop complaints in their tracks
and remember the blessings you have.*

Great Leaps

Do not despise these small beginnings,
for the Lord rejoices to see the work begin.

ZECHARIAH 4:10 NLT

Small beginnings are where we put consistency to work. When we begin with what we have and know to do, we are moving forward. May we recognize that our dreams will not become reality by wishful thinking. Instead, may we move with purposeful consistency toward our goals in small, actionable steps.

God does not despise small beginnings, so neither should we. He rejoices in every movement we make with faith, endurance, and vision. Transformation happens in the movement of our choices. Let us not overlook the little ways that we can implement the values of the kingdom of God into our lives. Every small surrender matters. Every choice is an opportunity. Instead of getting overwhelmed by the big picture today, take the time to consider small ways you can implement change and then do them.

Focus on where you are and what you can do today.

Everything Matters

Do you have the gift of speaking? Then speak as though God himself were speaking through you. Do you have the gift of helping others? Do it with all the strength and energy that God supplies. Then everything you do will bring glory to God through Jesus Christ. All glory and power to him forever and ever! Amen.

1 PETER 4:11 NLT

The talents we have are gifts from God. They are not afterthoughts from him but given to us with purpose and intention. There is beauty in the development of our talents. We do not need to deny the draw of our passions. We don't need to pretend to struggle with learning things that come easily to us. Humility is not denying our aptitude. We can be confident in our abilities and still not feel superior to others.

God made you with specific talents and unique abilities to see the world as you do. Whatever it is that you are drawn to, let love guide you in your growth. Do you love to sing? Sing with gratitude to the Lord. Do you love to help others? Do it with the strength of God's compassion moving you. Do you love to weave stories? Tell them with an open heart that expresses the goodness of God.

Whatever you are good at, do it with joy and love for God.

Creation's Story

You are worthy, our Lord and God, to receive glory and honor and power, for you created all things, and by your will they were created and have their being.

REVELATION 4:11 NIV

All creation reveals the glory of God. There is beauty in the sun rising over a mountain range. There is wonder in the way that a flower opens toward the light. The rhythms of the seasons reflect the rhythms of our lives. There is growth, there is death, and there is rebirth.

May we not neglect the opportunity to know God through the world around us. There is so much beauty! There is such intricacy in the ecosystems of nature. Instead of just rushing through the routine of your day, take time to engage with the world around you. Notice how the sunlight filters through your window. Take note of the new life springing around you. Revel in the beauty that is near, and let your heart respond as it will.

Look for God's beauty and creativity in the natural world.

God Is Love

No one has ever seen God.
But if we love each other, God lives in us,
and his love is brought to full expression in us.

1 JOHN 4:12 NLT

Love is an ever-flowing river from the heart of God. It rushes from the source of his being. Love is always the greatest choice that we can make. We do not reflect God when we make excuses for why our lack of love is acceptable. When we choose to extend kindness toward others, it is a gift that we give away.

Each of us receives freely from the love of God in unending measure. Choosing to love someone who has hurt us does not mean that there is no accountability for that person. Love does not excuse abuse. It is not a spiritual bypass for natural consequences. It does not mean open access to our lives. There is freedom in the love of God. It is always an invitation, and it is always our choice. May we dive deeper into the heart of God where we will receive increasing revelation of the power of his love.

Choose love over offense whenever you can.

Respectable

People who are not believers will respect the way you live, and you will not need to depend on others.

1 Thessalonians 4:12 NLT

How we live our lives matters. The fruit of our lives will reflect what we allow to feed us. Are we nourished by the love of God, feeding the seeds of his righteousness as we grow in him? Today is a good day to reflect on the values that inform our lives. Integrity, honesty, peacemaking, justice—the list could go on.

Consider the core values that you live according to. Look at your daily, weekly, and monthly routines. Do they line up with what you say is most important to you? It does not need to be complicated; your life does not need a complete overhaul. Simply refocus today and consider how you can take steps toward living the kind of life that matters to you. What do you want others to say about you? What are the things that you want to be clearly seen in your lifestyle and choices?

Look for how you can honor God and others with your choices.

Unmatched Wisdom

The word of God is living and active and sharper than any two-edged sword, and piercing as far as the division of soul and spirit, of both joints and marrow, and able to judge the thoughts and intentions of the heart.

HEBREWS 4:12 NASB

The wisdom of God cuts through the fog of our confusion with the light of clarity. When God reveals the truth of his Spirit, it is often simple and yet profoundly impactful. In the Scriptures, there is wisdom to teach us, guide us, and correct us. The Spirit of God brings deep revelation of the truths of God's nature and kingdom ways.

The Word of God is as active in our lives as it was in the life and ministry of Jesus. There is deeper understanding to discover, mysteries that he reveals to us in fellowship of Spirit to spirit. Let us look to him over and above the wisdom of this world. Though we may find some answers to questions we have in great thinkers, even they only know in part. But God is full of perfect wisdom to instruct, lead, and transform us.

Spend time in God's Word and meditate on a chosen passage throughout the day.

Nothing Is Wasted

Rejoice inasmuch as you participate in the sufferings of Christ, so that you may be overjoyed when his glory is revealed.

1 PETER 4:13 NIV

Suffering is not always a punishment for our sin. It is not an indictment of our shame. When we reduce it to such, we confuse the nature of God with our meager attempts to understand why we are experiencing pain. Jesus made it clear that we would suffer in this life. Jesus suffered, too!

Though we cannot escape loss, devastation, and grief in this life, we have a comforter who never leaves us. He is our constant confidant, our covering of love, and the one who holds us in our weeping. No seeds sown in tears are wasted. The pain we experience in this life is not to be ignored, but it is also not meant to be our full focus. Christ meets us in the midst of our messy emotions, and he holds us together. He will restore what is lost, and he will redeem what no person could dream of bringing back to life. Let us look to the one who never leaves, never turns away, and who always leans in close.

Turn your discouragement into gratitude by thanking God for being with you in it.

Seen and Known

Nothing in all creation is hidden from God's sight.
Everything is uncovered and laid bare before the eyes
of him to whom we must give account.

HEBREWS 4:13 NIV

God sees everything. He sees all that goes on in the world.
Even more, he sees the motive of every heart. He knows
what makes us tick, and he sees what causes us pain.
There is nothing that escapes his notice. May we know the
comfort of God as sovereign. He doesn't miss a thing!

There is so much in life that we cannot control. We don't
need to manipulate outcomes to ensure that we will get
what we feel we deserve. The Lord does not need our
attempts at regulating people or systems. This is not to
say that we should not work to see his kingdom come to
earth as it is in heaven. We are partners with him. Still, the
outcome is his. Let's remember that he is God, and he will
do what we could never do on our own. Let's trust him
above all else.

Trust God to account for all things
and let go of what you cannot control.

Springs of Refreshment

"If anyone drinks the living water I give them, they will never be thirsty again. For when you drink the water I give you, it becomes a gushing fountain of the Holy Spirit, flooding you with endless life!"

JOHN 4:14 TPT

The truth of Jesus is satisfying. His love is complete and without hidden agenda. It does not seek to manipulate us. It does not look to conform us into carbon copies of each other. His love sets us free to be the most liberated versions of ourselves that we can be. When we come alive in the love of Christ, we are empowered to make choices in line with his kingdom values.

His love springs up within us like a continual fountain. His Spirit in us feeds us from the fresh waters of his mercy every single day. Each moment is an opportunity to drink from the living waters of Christ. What he offers, nothing else compares to. What he gives is an everlasting expression of compassion. It satisfies our souls and expands our capacities to know, choose, and love him.

Meditate on the wonderful promises of Jesus.

Abundantly More

All of this is for your benefit. And as God's grace reaches more and more people, there will be great thanksgiving, and God will receive more and more glory.

2 CORINTHIANS 4:15 NLT

Have you ever been so grateful for a new discovery that you shared it with everyone you could think of? When our lives are impacted in wonderful ways by the addition of simple tools, do we not freely share our excitement with others? Every time God moves in grace toward us, may we make a point of thanking him and sharing his goodness.

No matter the extent to which you've understood God's grace, there is more for you! There is more than enough for everyone. God receives glory as we share our blessings with others. May we learn to give generously and to share what we have with others. It is for our good and for the glory of God every time that we do.

Share an experience of your gratitude toward God with someone today.

He Gets It

He understands humanity, for as a Man, our magnificent
King-Priest was tempted in every way just as we are,
and conquered sin.

HEBREWS 4:15 TPT

There is no human experience that Jesus does not relate
to. He is aware of our weakness in more than theory and
observation. When he put on the confines of humanity, he
experienced the same vulnerability that we all do. He knew
what it was to be thirsty and to feel hunger. He needed
sleep and rest in order to recharge his body. He grew
impatient at times. He relates to us fully in our weakness,
and we can trust that when he instructs us in his wisdom, it
is not outside of the possibilities of his grace and strength.

Instead of wallowing in our shame, we can come to Jesus
with the reality of our struggles. He will not turn us away.
He conquered sin and death for us! He did the heavy lifting.
Let us give up the striving on our own merit and abilities
and let the empowering grace of his presence guide,
strengthen, and help us in our weakness.

*Share your temptations with Jesus
and keep your heart open to his mercy.*

Living Love

We know how much God loves us, and we have put our
trust in his love. God is love, and all who live in love live
in God, and God lives in them.

1 John 4:16 NLT

When we live in the understanding of how deeply God
loves us, we cannot help but to be filled with this same
love for others. His love is large, and it is always expanding.
Where we are small in our caring, Jesus breaks the barriers
of our limits with his powerful tide of mercy. Choosing to
love is a choice to live in the reality of the living power of
God in us.

Do you know how much God loves you? Do you believe it?
If you automatically think of conditions of exception from
his love, than there is room to receive more of his affection.
Start with what you believe about yourself. Ask God to
reveal what he thinks of you. Jesus is your perfection. The
Father loves you as completely as he loves his Son. From
a place of deep acceptance, you can learn to love others
more fully.

*Write a letter of love and appreciation to someone you
deeply care for.*

A Fresh Start

Let us then with confidence draw near to the throne of grace, that we may receive mercy and find grace to help in time of need.

HEBREWS 4:16 ESV

Every day is a fresh opportunity to receive God's mercy. In our need, there is abundant grace for us. There is no need to drag our feet in despair when the living love of God is reaching toward us. The compassion of God never recedes. It is not like a tide that comes and goes. It is like a rushing waterfall, a gushing river, or a flowing fountain. May we receive what we need in the powerful presence of God today.

All that we need is found in fellowship with the Lord. This moment is a fresh start. May we not brush past this opportunity; let's take hold of the moment and press into the grace of our present strength. He is so very good.

Make a fresh start with someone you love in the same way you've received it from the Lord.

No Comparison

We view our slight, short-lived troubles in the light of eternity. We see our difficulties as the substance that produces for us an eternal, weighty glory far beyond all comparison.

2 CORINTHIANS 4:17 TPT

It can be disorienting when the demands of life sweep us up. There are seasons of life where there is too much to do in a day, too many requests to keep up with, and not enough time to savor the joys we wish would last longer. The difficulty of stress can weigh us down and distract us from the goodness present.

Come to Jesus with your to-do lists, your responsibilities, and your weariness. He can handle all of it. Ask him for his perspective on your present reality. Ask for his wisdom to help you with prioritization and time management. Look to him for relief and look to him for rest. There is so much good ahead, more beauty than you can yet imagine. In God's kingdom, there is abundance, there is light, and there is joy!

Think about your best day, and then let your heart dream about the all-surpassing goodness of God's kingdom.

May

Rejoice always, pray continually,
give thanks in all circumstance;
for this is God's will for you
in Christ Jesus.

1 THESSALONIANS 5:16-18 NIV

Indescribable Goodness

Such love has no fear, because perfect love expels
all fear. If we are afraid, it is for fear of punishment,
and this shows that we have not fully experienced
his perfect love.

1 JOHN 4:18 NLT

The love of God is more powerful than any other force in
this world. It is greater than fear, it is more potent than
hate, and it is constantly pushing back the boundaries
of our limited understanding. When we are afraid, it is
not because of the Lord. Countless times in his Word, he
instructed his followers to not be afraid, but to trust him.

When we are awaiting punishment for our slip-ups and
failures, we cannot move in the true freedom of God's love.
He sets us free to transform and grow up in his wisdom
without fear of failure. He corrects us, to be sure, but even
his correction builds us up rather than tears us down.
He breaks the power of lies over our thought patterns. It
can be disorienting, but with it comes greater ability to
recognize the indescribable goodness of his love. He is
always better than we can imagine.

*Reevaluate how you relate to God. Is it with fear
of punishment or in the embrace of his love?*

Better Things Ahead

We don't look at the troubles we can see now;
rather, we fix our gaze on things that cannot be seen.
For the things we see now will soon be gone,
but the things we cannot see will last forever.

2 CORINTHIANS 4:18 NLT

When we spend the majority of our time with our attention turned to our current troubles, it can be difficult to imagine a better tomorrow. Let us learn how to let go of the need to make sense of our trials and instead look to Jesus for his eternal wisdom. Let us fix our focus, not on what is obvious, but on what is true and lasting.

Though troubles will come and go, the faithfulness of God's love can never be interrupted. There are no shortages of his kindness, and his presence is fully with us through every high and low of this life. May we focus on the everlasting goodness of God and on the promise of what is to come in the fullness of God's kingdom on earth as it is in heaven.

Focus on the things that truly matter today.

Our Reason

We love because he first loved us.

1 John 4:19 nrsv

Jesus' mandate for us to love one another is not an easy task. It does not come naturally for us to interact with those who despise us with mercy and kindness. It is not instinctive for us to turn our other cheek to the one who first slapped us. The love of Jesus goes far beyond what is convenient and acceptable.

When we are struggling to be kind with those we cannot stand, may we remember that our love is not agreement with their choices. That does not even weigh in. Love does not look for reasons to extend toward others. The mercy of God is a force that moves without expectation of what can be returned. We love because of how lavishly we have been loved by Jesus. His love is our source, our strength, and our movement. He is our reason. He is all the reason we ever need.

Be the first to extend kindness to someone you have struggled to get along with.

All You Need

This same God who takes care of me will supply all your needs from his glorious riches, which have been given to us in Christ Jesus.

PHILIPPIANS 4:19 NLT

Instead of letting random thoughts rush around your head, take stock of your needs by writing them down. Get out a piece of paper and write down the thoughts that keep returning to your attention. It may be helpful to write a to-do list. Also, feel free to write down the worries that come to mind. What are your needs? What are the problems you face?

After you have written them, take time to consider solutions. Perhaps some are simple while others require more strategy. Ask God for wisdom in how to proceed and record the ideas that come to mind. Before you return to your day, take time to account for already answered prayers and for the blessings you have. Start a gratitude list next to the other. Remember to look at it often and add to it as you think of more reasons to be thankful.

Thank God for his provision.

More Than Words

The kingdom of God
does not consist in words
but in power.

1 CORINTHIANS 4:20 NASB

The power of God is so much greater than belief in ideologies. It is the power that makes deaf ears hear, that mends broken bones and hearts, that breathes life and hope into disappointment and despair. The words of others do not define lives. Though what we say is important, how we live is much more indicative of our guiding values.

The kingdom of God is more than sentiment. It is not made up of words that weave a story, no matter how beautiful it sounds. The kingdom of God exists in the power of God. It is in the being of God. It is the love of God, incarnate. It is the resurrection power of Christ. It is more than words can express. Let us look to the faithfulness of God, the power of his mercy at work in our world and our lives. Let us not reduce the kingdom of God to a nice idea. Instead, let us look at how the wonder-working power of his love moves in real ways.

*Recognize where mystery meets wonder
and thank God for his power.*

Renewed Perspective

Let the Spirit renew your thoughts and attitudes.

EPHESIANS 4:23 NLT

It is important to evaluate our thoughts on a regular basis. Not all that we think is reality, nor is it necessarily based in the truth of God's Word. There are traditions we adopt simply because we were conditioned to believe them. There are cultural ideas that were implanted within our psyches from our upbringings. Just because we think something does not make it right or true.

When we are presented with new information, may we let the Spirit of wisdom broaden our understanding. Critical thinking is a gift because it allows us to separate ourselves from our thoughts. It allows us to question why we believe what we do. With the Spirit as our help, wisdom enlarges our understanding of his love rather than reducing us to falling in line with small thinking. Let's allow the Spirit to renew our thoughts in the truth of God's unlimited power and unmatched mercy.

Don't believe everything you think. Instead, let the Spirit challenge and renew your thoughts in his truth.

It's Time

"The time is coming—indeed it's here now—when true worshipers will worship the Father in spirit and in truth. The Father is looking for those who will worship him that way."

JOHN 4:23 NLT

When you think about worship, what comes to mind? Is it a church service with singing and raised hands? Is it music that moves your heart? Is it feeding the widow and the orphan? The worship that the Father is looking for is surrendered lives. He wants our love on display. When we yield our hearts to him, we give him leadership of our lives, and we know that he always guides us in the power of his mercy.

What would it look like for you to worship the Father in spirit and truth with your life today? Look for new ways to offer worship to him. If you normally sing your praises to him, sing a new song with your own words. If you dance before him, find a new rhythm and move your body in a different way. If you encourage others, find creative ways to do it. Don't stop there! Stretch your imagination in how worship can be displayed in your daily life.

Worship the Lord with your choices today.

Healer

Jesus was going throughout all Galilee, teaching in their synagogues and proclaiming the gospel of the kingdom, and healing every kind of disease and every kind of sickness among the people.

MATTHEW 4:23 NASB

Jesus was not simply a great teacher or rabbi in the days of his ministry. He moved in the power of God, reaching people with the tangible love of God in signs and wonders. He healed broken bodies, driving sickness from those who were ill. The gospel of his kingdom is still revealed through the power of God meeting us in miracles.

May we refuse to stay small in our prayer lives, even when we don't have answers to questions of why and how God moves in the way he does. Instead of letting disappointment weigh down our hearts, may we press into the substantial presence of God with us. Jesus is still a healer. He is still the raiser of the dead. He is the resurrected one, and his power is as potent today as it was when he walked this earth.

Pray for someone's healing today.

Listen

"Those who listen with open hearts will receive more revelation. But those who don't listen with open hearts will lose what little they think they have!"

MARK 4:25 TPT

Humility lends to our growth. When we recognize that we don't have it all together and we don't know all there is to know, we see the humanity in each other without need for categorization or comparison. The soil of our hearts is ready for the nourishment of God's wisdom.

Instead of seeking to be heard today, let us instead look to listen. Let's tune our hearts and ears to hear what is behind the words that others speak. Let's not listen with intent to respond, but with intent to understand. When we look past what we know of people into their experiences, compassion has room to grow. May we be lovers of God who listen well to his voice and to the cries of others. There is always more to learn, and what a wonderful opportunity we have to do that today!

Practice being a good listener today.

Love in Action

This is the love of God,
that we keep his commandments.
And his commandments are not burdensome.

1 JOHN 5:3 ESV

The commands of God, as laid out in the words and teachings of Jesus, are not rigid rules to mindlessly abide by. How we live our lives matters; the choices we make will lead us in certain trajectories. The love of God is all-consuming, and it covers every part of our lives. It is powerful to transform us into the likeness of God. It is able to move us in ways that we would never move ourselves.

God does not require what he does not already provide. Our hope is in him because he is our living hope. Our salvation is in his resurrection life, not in our ability to comprehend his power. His love is the source of our own. He pours out what we are required to offer others. What a gracious gift this is! All that we need is already found in abundance in him. Let's drink deeply from the waters of his living love and live out of that overflow today, following his ways and Word.

Obey the Lord's leading through his Word.

Unashamed

Hope does not put us to shame, because God's love has been poured into our hearts through the Holy Spirit who has been given to us.

ROMANS 5:5 ESV

In darkness, the hope of a new day dawning is not in vain. It is not foolishness to recognize that what we currently experience will pass. Every moment moves into the next as days progress into years. May we live with hope as our anthem, looking forward to the promises that God has made. He is faithful, and he will always fulfill his Word.

Have you ever wanted to pull someone back into reality when you heard them speak of the future with hope? Have you ever been ashamed of thinking too positively about God's provision? The Holy Spirit is with you now, so take advantage of the gift of his presence. God is with you; he will encourage, strengthen, and comfort you. He is everything you need. When your hope is in him, it will never be put to shame.

Let hope rise without trying to temper it in yourself or others.

Satisfied

*"Blessed are those who hunger and thirst
for righteousness, for they will be filled."*

MATTHEW 5:6 NRSV

What has been the driving force behind your days? What have you been working toward these last months? What vision has kept you moving this last year? With a little thoughtfulness, consider what you have hungered and thirsted for more than any other thing. Has it been to be present with your family? Has it been to move forward in your career? These are worthy pursuits. Take a step further and look at what undergirds that drive. Look at the whys beneath the what.

It is not too basic a desire to want to love others well. It is not too simple to want to be able to affect change in the world through endeavors of justice. May you be encouraged as you look under the surface of your desires. May you find the pull of God's love leading you. And if you don't, you get to choose differently today and realign your values in the light of God's present and overwhelming mercy.

*Make an intention to be satisfied
by God's presence with you.*

Let Go of Worry

Pour out all your worries and stress upon him and leave them there, for he always tenderly cares for you.

1 Peter 5:7 tpt

As long as the sun rises and sets, there will be unexpected challenges that come our way. We can't anticipate how every detail of our lives will play out. We can't know the troubles that the future holds. And yet, we have fellowship with a faithful God. Nothing surprises him! He knows exactly how to tend to us in every season of our lives.

Instead of letting the stress of our anxious thoughts weigh us down today, let's give them over to the Lord. We find true rest in the peace of his presence. We find our belonging in the confidence of his love. He has not failed us, and he never will. Let his unwavering mercy hold you today as you give him the weight of your worries. He will tend to your needs and take care of you. There's no need to surrender to anxiety, for the one who called you is faithful to lead you into his goodness.

Give God your worries today.
Rest in his love.

Settled by Grace

May the God of all grace, who called us to His eternal glory by Christ Jesus, after you have suffered a while, perfect, establish, strengthen, and settle you.

1 PETER 5:10 NKJV

Though we may suffer grief, pain, and loss, the Lord will never abandon us in our weakness. He is close in comfort and near in our undoing, and he holds us together. He is the God of all grace, not the God of some. He has more than enough power to perfect, fill, establish, strengthen, and settle us. He does not leave us to waste away in our suffering.

May the God of all grace fill you with his lavish mercy today. Yesterday was not the end of your story, and today is not, either. Look over your history with God. Do you see how he delivered you from what was once overwhelming to you? He is with you in the valleys as well as the heights. Wherever you are, he is already there. Take heart and take hope in his present nearness today.

Acknowledge where God's love has brought beauty out of your troubles.

Even Greater

If while we were still enemies, God fully reconciled
us to himself through the death of his Son, then
something greater than friendship is ours. Now that
we are at peace with God, and because we share in his
resurrection life, how much more we will be rescued
from sin's dominion!

ROMANS 5:10 TPT

Moses was known as a friend to God. David was known as
a man after God's own heart. Abraham was the father of
nations. Jesus, the Son of God, paved a new path for us. He
showed us the way to worship the Father in spirit and in
truth, to live as overcomers in this world, and to walk in the
confidence of God's affection.

We have peace with God through Christ. There is no
striving in this love. There is nothing more that we could
offer the Father than what Jesus has already given. We
come into alignment with his merciful heart when we come
to Jesus with open hearts and surrendered lives. With
Christ as our leader, there is more than friendship with
God. We have been adopted as sons and daughters of the
Living God, and our souls have come alive in him.

*Extend peace to others from the peace of God
that is already yours.*

Built Up

Encourage one another and build one another up, just as you are doing.

1 THESSALONIANS 5:11 ESV

There is incredible strength in the encouragement we give and receive from others. When we call out the goodness of God we see in each other, our spirits are strengthened in purpose. We should look for ways to build each other up in love whenever we have the opportunity. The kingdom of God is one of abundance, so let's give away reassurance the way that God gives us his mercy.

Are you known as an encourager? Do your friends know what you appreciate about them? Does your family know what it is that you love about them? May you take the opportunities before you and build others up in the love of God. Think of a time when you received encouragement that reinforced your resolve. We all need reassurance when we are persevering through this life. Be a voice of hope and courage for someone today.

Call a friend and encourage them.

Confident Communion

Since we have this confidence, we can also have great boldness before him, for if we ask anything agreeable to his will, he will hear us.

1 JOHN 5:14 TPT

We have been brought near to the heart of God through fellowship with Christ. We are not at a distance, and we don't need to wonder whether he hears us. Just as surely as we are known by God, we have his attention. We don't have to compete with others for an audience before him, for his capacity is endless.

Take courage as you come to Jesus today. He sees you as you are, and he accepts you in his love. There is nothing you could offer him that he would be shocked by. There is nothing you could say to deter his mercy. Give him all that you are, and his love will reach the depths of your soul. Be bold in your prayers today, asking for more than you have. There's no need to filter yourself with God. He loves it when you come to him!

Pray without a filter today.

Beyond Description

The Lord's greatness is beyond description,
and he deserves all the praise that comes to him.
He is our King-God,
and it's right to be in holy awe of him.

PSALM 96:4 TPT

Have you taken time to think about God's goodness lately? When was the last time you let your imagination run wild with the possibilities of his wonderful love? Though we cannot hold the magnitude of his greatness with our understanding, the Spirit gives us revelations of his goodness that increase our comprehension.

Try to describe how good the Lord is, how vast his love is, or how powerful his resurrection life is, and you may be at a loss for words. When awe sets in, no words can sum up the feeling. There is an expansion within us, our souls simultaneously reaching out and letting in the wonder of God beyond space and time. He is greater than we can describe, and yet he is close and mindful of us. What a wonder!

*Spend time doing something
that cultivates awe within you.*

Fresh Start

If anyone is in Christ, he is a new creation.
The old has passed away;
behold, the new has come.

1 CORINTHIANS 5:17 ESV

Today is a fresh start for you. Take this moment as an opportunity to let go of the past that you cannot change. Breathe in hope as you look ahead to that which you cannot control. Here and now, in the middle of your reality, is where God is working. Take rest in his presence and take courage in his ability to make all things new in him.

Christ is the beginning and the end. He is endlessly creative in his workmanship. He is full of clarity and wisdom for every problem you face. When you are stumped for how to move ahead in any area of life, he knows the best way to go. Lean into his presence and listen for his voice. He is faithful to guide you through the ups and downs of this life. Your life is covered by his mercy that makes all things new.

If there is a piece of your past where shame has a hold on you, leave it in the hands of Jesus today.

Fresh Air

If anyone is in Christ, there is a new creation:
everything old has passed away;
see, everything has become new!

2 Corinthians 5:17 nrsv

It is an amazing truth to know that Christ has made us new in his living love. We have been purified in his cleansing flow. We have been given a fresh slate, a new opportunity to choose how we will live. The old systems and patterns of our lives do not dictate how our futures will go. By the overcoming power of God's love, we are transformed into vessels of his mercy where old is made new and broken is made whole.

If you are in Christ, you have hope. This hope is not only for some day in the future; it is for your transformation here and now. With the turning of seasons from winter to spring, hope is revived as we watch dormant things come back to life. There is new growth, and this mirrors our lives in Christ. May we look for where life is springing in new ways today. Surely, it is there!

Spend some time in nature today.

In Everything

In everything give thanks;
for this is God's will for you in Christ Jesus.

1 THESSALONIANS 5:18 NASB

Gratitude comes more easily when it comes to what benefits us. It is not a natural reaction to hardship to turn around and thank God for it. Yet, this is good practice for our souls. When we learn to give thanks in all things, we are able to recognize that no matter how hard the circumstance, God is able to restore, redeem, instruct, and grow us. Though he may not send the storm, he is faithful in the midst of it.

Will you let this instruction of Paul be your aim for today? "In everything give thanks." There is beauty in expressing gratitude to God, no matter what our present troubles are. He remains unchanging in love and undeterred in justice. He is faithful, he is true, and he is able to turn our mourning into dancing. He is the God of redemption. He is the God of our great jubilation! In everything, give thanks.

*Practice saying thank you to God throughout your day,
no matter the circumstance.*

Reunions of Mercy

God has made all things new,
and reconciled us to himself,
and given us the ministry
of reconciling others to God.

2 Corinthians 5:18 tpt

What is the ministry of reconciliation and what does it look like? In plainer language, it is sharing the gospel of Christ with others. Jesus has resolved the separation between God and humankind; he is the way, the truth, and the life. We come to the Father through him. We have found our peace with God, and he longs for every person to be free in his love.

In a world full of lines that keep pushing people to divide, the cross of Christ is unifying. His love is inclusive. It calls to the people on the edges and welcomes them in. There is no one that it excludes. May we look like the love that has beckoned us by doing the same as Jesus. May we welcome all in the name of Christ, without disqualifying people based on what they look like or what their lives have been. His love levels the playing field for all of us.

Take steps to unify others rather than allowing divisions to drive people further apart.

Powerful Name

Give thanks for everything to God the Father
in the name of our Lord Jesus Christ.

EPHESIANS 5:20 NLT

When we treat each day as the gift it is, we are able to
more readily find the small blessings hidden in our lives.
Cultivating a heart of gratitude allows us to hear birdsong,
take in a sunset, and revel in laughter with the perception
that these are each gifts of goodness. In Christ, we have
hope. In Christ, we have peace. In Christ, we have joy. In
Christ, we have more than enough.

What simple joys bring you satisfaction? Is it conversation
with a good friend that knows you without explanation?
Is it the companionship of a loyal pet? Is it the way the
evening light reflects off the water? Whatever it is that
brings you joy, give thanks to God. Let the name of Jesus
be on your lips throughout your day and thank him for the
mercies that are present in your life.

Remember Jesus throughout your day.

Today Is the Day

God says, "At just the right time, I heard you.
On the day of salvation, I helped you."
Indeed, the "right time" is now.
Today is the day of salvation.

2 CORINTHIANS 6:2 NLT

Timing matters. Though we may be impatient to get from point A to point B, the journey between the two prepares us for what is to come. As long as we are living, the present moment is all that we have control over. We can make our choices and set our trajectories, but we cannot account for the unexpected troubles that will arise. But God knows. He sees.

God is our ever-present help in times of trouble. He is our deliverer and our Savior. He is always with those who look to him for help. May you know the confidence of his presence today. This is the time that you have been waiting for; the fullness of his presence is yours. Every moment is an opportunity to lean into the abundant grace of his strength. The right time to look to him is right now. This is it. Lean in.

Treat today as the only day that matters.

Spring Rains

"Let us acknowledge the Lord;
let us press on to acknowledge him.
As surely as the sun rises,
he will appear;
he will come to us like the winter rains,
like the spring rains that water the earth."

HOSEA 6:3 NIV

When we learn to acknowledge the Lord in all ways for all things, our hearts grow in the practice of gratitude. Let us not grow tired of looking for ways to recognize the Lord in our lives. He is more faithful than the sunrise. He is more reliable than the changing of the seasons. He is glorious, and he is always at work in us.

The Lord is with us, but we know that the fullness of his coming is still not here. His Spirit is at work with the power of his mighty mercy right now. He moves like the wind, and we can see the effects of his goodness. Yet, a day is coming when we will see him face to face. Until that day comes, let us look for the ways that he faithfully shows himself in the world around us.

Thank God for today's weather.

Satisfaction in Simplicity

True godliness with contentment
is itself great wealth.

1 TIMOTHY 6:6 NLT

There is tremendous beauty and satisfaction in finding serenity in the present moment. Perfection and ease may not be possible in every season of the soul, but contentment is. With our hearts surrendered to the love of God, following his ways and his leading, we have the fullness of his presence. There is always a reason to celebrate his present goodness, for he is our abundant portion.

Look for simple joys throughout your day and give thanks for each one you find. Even in the harshest circumstances, there is light. Even in the darkest night, the stars shine bright. There is living water to quench your thirst. There is nourishment for your soul in the Word of God. There is fresh air to breathe, sun to warm your skin, and there is hope in the rains of spring. Look for where mercy meets you, and you will find the fingerprints of God in your life.

Be grateful for the choices you can make today.

Faithful Father

"Your Father knows exactly what you need
even before you ask him!"

MATTHEW 6:8 NLT

The same God who provides shelter and sustenance for animals in the wild is the God who provides for our every need. He knows exactly what we require before we are even aware of the need. We can lay our worries down at his feet and trust him to provide what we cannot provide for ourselves.

Even so, let us reflect his generous goodness in the ways that we interact with others in this life. When we see others in need, let's be the hands and feet of Jesus. As we partner with his kindness, giving to others with no regard for the potential of return, we reflect the mercy of God toward us. Whether it is buying a meal for someone in need or taking time to help them carry their groceries, let us look for ways to meet the needs of others as God does for us.

Look for ways to meet someone else's need today.

Humble Justice

He has told you, O man, what is good,
and what does the LORD require of you.
But to do justice, and to love kindness,
and to walk humbly with your God.

MICAH 6:8 ESV

God is full of justice, and he will make all wrong things right. He does not ignore the cries of the oppressed, and he will not let abusers get away with taking advantage of the vulnerable. As we humbly walk with our God, letting his love transform us from the inside out, his heartbeat becomes the rhythm we live by.

Let us be known as people who love kindness and who choose love over every other competing driving force. Compassion coupled with humility is the way of the cross. As we learn to love justice, advocating for those who are taken advantage of, we press further into the fierce passion of God's affection. Let us be people who press into love more and more and throw every excuse for apathy to the side. He is worthy of our surrender, and love is worth the cost of our pride and comfort.

Stand up for someone today.

And Yet

Our hearts ache, but we always have joy.
We are poor, but we give spiritual riches to others.
We own nothing, and yet we have everything.

2 Corinthians 6:10 NLT

In the tension of the in-between, we can find peace. Though our hearts ache with loss, the joy of the Lord is still present. Though we may be poor in this world, we have abundance of spiritual wealth to offer others. Though we may not have much to physically offer, we have all that we need in the communion of Christ within us.

Jesus is the source of our life. He is the living water that satisfies our souls. He is the fire that burns away excess distractions that keep us from love. He is the refreshing fountain that continually cleanses us in his righteousness. He is the fullness of everything we long for in this life. He is the perfect parent, the most loving partner, and the best friend we could ever have. No matter what we lack, we have more than enough in him.

Remember what you already have when you are distracted by lack today.

Freedom over Fear

Sin is no longer your master, for you no longer live under the requirements of the law. Instead, you live under the freedom of God's grace.

ROMANS 6:14 NLT

What does it look like to live free from fear? God has not called you to be enslaved to perfection in the law. You cannot earn his favor, and his love does not shame your mistakes or missteps. His grace is so much greater than your failures. His love drives out the power of fear that keeps you from moving forward. His love frees you to move without the worry of getting it wrong.

Stay close to the love of the Lord, letting it lead you, and you will find that freedom is sweeter than you could imagine. The grace of God gives you the permission to live with love as the banner over your life. When you mess up, he is there to teach you, brush you off, and guide you. There is no need to let fear dictate your decisions any longer. Be free! Christ has given you complete freedom in him.

When you recognize fear ruling a decision, give it to God, lay it aside, and use your freedom to choose better.

Sons and Daughters

"I will be a father to you,
and you shall be sons and daughters to Me,"
says the Lord Almighty.

2 CORINTHIANS 6:18 NASB

God is a good father. In fact, he is the best Father. There are no hidden motives in his heart, and his love completely covers us at all times. He is not impatient or hasty. He does not lose his temper or storm away when we throw our accusations at him. He always makes time for us, and we do not need to compete for his attention. He is the perfect one, and we will always find a welcome embrace when we turn to him.

As children, we are dependent on our caregivers to feed, protect, and clothe us. We are helpless when we come into this world, and we are helpless when we leave it. A good parent does not simply give their child the necessities; they also provide a safe space to grow, play, and flourish. May we look for the goodness in our relationship with our parents, removing the expectation for perfection and replacing it with the beauty of lived-out love.

Thank a parent or parental figure for how they have impacted your life.

June

The Lord is my strength and shield.
I trust him with all my heart.
He helps me, and my heart is filled with joy.
I burst out in songs of thanksgiving.

PSALM 28:7 NLT

Nothing Hidden

"Your Father, whom you cannot see, will see you.
Your Father sees what is done in secret,
and he will reward you."

MATTHEW 6:18 NCV

What we do in the moments that go unnoticed by others is as important as our choices and interactions when we are clearly seen. The Father doesn't miss a single movement of sacrifice. He sees every act of love we make. What is done in secret is plain to him, and he will not fail to reward us for the integrity we choose.

May we not give into the idea that the small things in life don't matter. How we choose to live when no one is watching is as important as how we present ourselves to others. May they be one and the same, for God is always watching. He is the one who keeps record of our surrender. May we not grow weary doing good, for it matters. May we live with honesty and transparency before the Lord and others, knowing that it keeps us humble and dependent on the grace of God as our strength.

Keep living with integrity.

In Due Time

"God blesses you who are hungry now,
for you will be satisfied.
God blesses you who weep now,
for in due time you will laugh."

LUKE 6:21 NLT

On hard days, when sadness washes over you and you cannot shake off discouragement, what is your response? Do you shame yourself for feeling down? Do you feel as though you are missing the mark? Happiness is not equivalent to godliness. God can handle your weakness. In fact, he invites it!

When you are weak, God will be your strength. Give him your honesty, the reality of your struggles when they arise. Let him take the weight of your worries and disappointment. He can handle them all. Nothing is too heavy for the Lord to carry. He does not want your false positivity; he wants you as you are. In all things, look to the Lord. He is near, and he will help you. He is not disappointed by your sadness. Turn to him, and you will find that he is humble, he is loving, and he is attuned to your heart.

Don't give up hope. Look to the Lord today.

Highly Valued

"Look at all the birds—do you think they worry about their existence? They don't plant or reap or store up food, yet your heavenly Father provides them each with food. Aren't you much more valuable to your Father than they?"

MATTHEW 6:26 TPT

If we can learn anything from nature, may it be that worry is unnecessary. Though we are prone to it, that does not mean that we must choose to live under its weight. Our minds are transformed in the power of Christ, and we are empowered by his grace to instead capture our thoughts and put them up to the light of his love.

Even more valuable than the birds of the air, the flowers of the field, or the beasts of the forest, we have been called children of the Most High God. We are highly valued by the King of kings and Lord of lords. The one who created the stars, the earth, and everything in the universe is the one who formed us. Let us look through the lens of his love today and see the value of each person we interact with today.

Give a small gift to someone you value.

Come and Rest

"Come away by yourselves to a secluded place and rest a while." (For there were many people coming and going, and they did not even have time to eat.)

MARK 6:31 NASB

Do you regard rest as a luxury? It is important to know that it is not. It is a necessity. How can you build rhythms of rest into your life? If you do not make it a priority, then it will not happen. God created the Sabbath, and he did it with purpose. He took a day to enjoy what he had created and to rest from work. He did it so that we would have an example to follow. May you know that rest is as godly as sacrifice. Don't neglect it, for it is for your benefit and your health.

The demands of life do not dissipate when business hours are over. There will always be more required of us than we have the capacity to give. Let us take the invitation that Jesus offers us, the same way he did with his disciples. "Come away...to a secluded place and rest awhile."

Carve out an hour in your day to lay aside responsibilities and truly rest.

Show Them

*"Show mercy and compassion for others,
just as your heavenly Father overflows
with mercy and compassion for all."*

LUKE 6:36 TPT

Jesus' instruction that we show mercy and compassion for others is a reminder that the nature of God the Father is full of love. He is kind to all, and he overflows with abundant mercy to all that he has made. How will those who do not know the love of God be introduced to it unless we live it out?

Paul asks us this question: "But how can people call on him for help if they've not yet believed? And how can they believe in one they've not yet heard of? (Romans 10:14)." How will people know that God is merciful and compassionate unless we show mercy and compassion? This is no small afterthought that Jesus spoke to his disciples. This is what it looks like to live the gospel of Christ. May we continue to receive the depths of his love and to live it out with generosity.

*Let compassion be the aim of your interactions
with others today.*

No Matter What

"All that the Father gives me will come to me,
and whoever comes to me I will never cast out."

JOHN 6:37 ESV

You have been called by love, chosen as a child of God,
and brought into a family where you are understood,
accepted, and completely loved. Come to Jesus and find
the satisfaction of fellowship with him. He will not cast you
out or turn you away. His kindness draws you in, and it will
do so every time you turn to him.

Consider that the same love Christ has for you, he has for
all. He loves those that you struggle to get along with. He
loves the brash and the broken. The pitiful and the proud
are all welcome to come to him, though the choice is theirs.
May you see through the perspective of his strong love as
you move about your day. Let his compassion fill and move
you. He is your faithful friend, constant companion, and
wise teacher.

Thank the Lord for his faithful presence in your life.

No More Judging

Jesus said, "Forsake the habit of criticizing and judging others, and then you will not be criticized and judged in return. Don't look at others and pronounce them guilty, and you will not experience guilty accusations yourself. Forgive over and over and you will be forgiven over and over."

LUKE 6:37 TPT

Criticism is not a fruit of the Spirit. Neither is judgment of others. If we spend our energy picking others apart, we miss the areas where we have yet to grow. None of us is perfect, though we are trying our best in life. With grace as our motto, may we offer each other the benefit of the doubt. May we choose to forgive, even when others refuse to change; it is for our benefit that we do!

When we live with patience, kindness, and peace, we allow room for others' humanity. May we set aside our unrealistic and perfectionistic standards of others and offer the humble love, instead. Let us consider how we want to be treated and treat others in that way. Do we want to be criticized and judged? Or do we want the opportunity to repair, restore, and transform?

When you begin to criticize someone in your heart today, invite grace to change your perspective.

Filled to Overflow

I am filled with comfort.
In all our affliction,
I am overflowing with joy.

2 Corinthians 7:4 esv

In the midst of deep grief, the Lord is still full of abundant love for you. May you be filled with the comfort of his presence. May you know the deep, abiding joy of his tender care. No matter the trial, no matter how deeply entrenched you are in pain, God is still the same powerful and merciful God that he has always been. The persistent peace of his presence is a deep well that will never run dry.

In days of relative calm, you will find the ground beneath your feet is steady. In moments of celebration, you will feel the depths of gratitude bubbling up again. Today, no matter where this finds you, turn to the Lord. He is abundant in kindness, and his peace surpasses your grasp of it. If you see someone struggling in their own pain, reach out and remind them that they are not alone.

Offer encouragement to someone who is struggling today.

Generations of Mercy

"Know therefore that the LORD your God is God;
he is the faithful God, keeping his covenant of love
to a thousand generations of those who love him
and keep his commandments."

DEUTERONOMY 7:9 NIV

Look throughout the Scriptures, and you will find evidence of God's faithfulness throughout the history of Israel. He was loyal to his people, helping them whenever they cried out to him. He brought them from the bondage of their slavery into the freedom of the promised land. Though they wandered away from him, he kept showing them mercy. He is the same now. God is full of kindness, and he continues to fulfill his promises today.

When was the last time you read a testimony of God's goodness in someone's life? When was the last time God's faithful love in another's story caused your heart to respond in openness and wonder? Today, reach out to someone who has walked with the Lord for a long time and ask them how God has been faithful to them. It will encourage your heart to think about what he can also do for you.

Acknowledge how God's faithfulness has played out through history.

Christ's Compassion

When the Lord saw her,
his heart overflowed with compassion.
"Don't cry!" he said.

LUKE 7:13 NLT

When you see someone who is suffering, what is your gut reaction? Is it to offer comfort? Is it to ignore them because it feels uncomfortable? Love should move us. It does not brush off another's pain because of our own discomfort. Jesus was moved with compassion by the sorrow he recognized in a mother's cries. He let compassion lead him and disrupt his schedule.

Grief is not convenient. It is not on a timeline. So, too, compassion as a response to another's suffering is not convenient. It involves sacrifice of time. When we allow compassion to redirect us, we offer more than our time; we offer our attention. Can you think back to a time when someone's compassion comforted you? In our grief, even the smallest acts of kindness can bring solace and hope. As we walk with the Lord, his love will lead us in directions we may have never anticipated. May we let his mercy guide us today.

Offer comfort to someone who is grieving a loss.

Continue

Each one of you should continue to live the way God has given you to live—the way you were when God called you.

1 CORINTHIANS 7:17 NCV

Have you ever felt like you needed to completely overhaul your life in order to serve God? Do you think that those who work in ministry or in the church are holier than those who work in various businesses? Though some are called to change their jobs in order to align with where they feel God is leading them, know that it isn't what you do that makes you a follower of God—it is how you live.

Keep your heart submitted to God and continue to work at what you are good at. You don't have to change careers to make a difference in the world. You just need to shine bright with the love of Christ. That can be done anywhere, anytime, in any role. Keep pursuing your hobbies and fanning the flame of your passion projects. Anything done with a yielded heart of love is holy.

Continue to offer God thanks through your submitted life.

Making Things Right

I will give all my thanks to you, Lord,
for you make everything right in the end.
I will sing my highest praise
to the God of the Highest Place!

PSALM 7:17 TPT

It is good for us to partner with God in bringing his kingdom to earth. It is right that we live our lives with love, reaching out in compassion to those around us. It is a beautiful movement of mercy for us to gather in those who have been pushed to the edges of society and to show them what God's kindness looks like. Even so, in all of our good deeds, God alone can right all the wrongs that remain.

It is not our striving in life that leads God to follow through on his promises. He is faithful, and he will always act that way because it is his nature. His loyalty is dependent upon him, not us. May we take courage and hope from the incomparable goodness of our God. May we pour out our thanks to him today, trusting that he will make everything right in the end.

Thank the Lord for his fulfilled promises.

Approved in Christ

There is therefore now no condemnation
for those who are in Christ Jesus.

ROMANS 8:1 ESV

In our hurt, we might throw accusations at others in order
to justify our shortcomings. In our weakness, we may find
that our fuses are short and our frustrations plentiful. It is
not easy to look past offense while using our own strength.
Fortunately, there is an abundance of grace in the presence
of God to help us in our relationships. There is more than
enough mercy to cover our failures in the same.

No matter how disappointed others may be in us, God
does not hold our failures against us. It is right that
we seek reconciliation in humble love, but let us first
recognize that when we turn to the Lord for forgiveness,
he completely cleanses us from our sin. There is nothing
that he holds against us because it has already been
covered in the powerful blood of Jesus. His love purifies us
completely.

Remember that God does not hold anything against you.

Nothing Impossible

This is what the LORD of Heaven's Armies says:
"All this may seem impossible to you now, a small
remnant of God's people. But is it impossible for me?"
says the LORD of Heaven's Armies.

ZECHARIAH 8:6 NLT

With the Lord, all things are possible. Have you ever looked
at a situation in your life and felt utterly at a loss? Though
you may not know what to do, God does. Even if you know
what it will take to change, you may not have the means to
do so. But God does! Everything is possible with God, for
he is the Creator of all things.

Try reframing your thoughts today when you are presented
with an overwhelming situation. Instead of letting
helplessness drive you to dread, get excited for what God
will do. He does not let anything in our lives go to waste.
He can do far more than you can even imagine him doing!
Pray and ask him for help, trusting him to follow through in
faithfulness.

Trust God with the impossible situations in your life.

Gracious Giving

You are rich in everything—in faith, in speaking, in knowledge, in truly wanting to help, and in the love you learned from us. In the same way, be strong also in the grace of giving.

2 Corinthians 8:7 NCV

When we let love guide our actions, we will find that our hearts overflow with the abundance of God's Spirit. Let us give our lives to gaining the riches of his kingdom, letting our ideas of worldly wealth become an afterthought. When we grow in God's wisdom, looking for ways to help others and moving through our lives with compassion, we spread seeds of the fruit of the Spirit.

Generosity is a core kingdom value. God freely gives out of the abundance of his love, and so should we. When we give away what we have, when we sacrifice our comfort in order to help another, we make room to receive more from the Lord. He always fills what is running dry. May we give graciously, reflecting the nature of our bighearted Father.

Buy a meal or beverage for someone today.

Extravagant Love

Many waters cannot quench love;
rivers cannot sweep it away.
If one were to give all the wealth of one's house for love,
it would be utterly scorned.

SONG OF SOLOMON 8:7 NIV

The love of God is more extravagant than we can imagine. It knows no beginning or end. It is larger than life. It is more powerful than the grave. It is infinitely better than we could ever put into words. Nothing can stop the love of God from reaching us, from overpowering our fears, or from overcoming our doubts. His love speaks a better word than the promises of mankind.

Let's allow the weight of our actions to display the depth of our love today. Instead of using words to describe what we feel, let us seek to show others in tangible ways how much we care for them. Thoughtfulness can go a long way to revealing our hearts. Words matter, but so does follow-through. Let's be people who look for ways to love others with creativity, just as God lavishes his love on us.

Show affection to a loved one.

Light of Life

"I am the Light of the world; he who follows Me will not walk in the darkness, but will have the Light of life."

JOHN 8:12 NASB

When we walk in the light, just as Jesus is in the light, we will not wander from his pure purposes. How do we do it? By following his loving lead and example. He draws us in with kindness, washing us in the purifying power of his love. As we open our hearts and lives to him, he fills us with his Spirit. He leads us in mercy, instructs us with his matchless wisdom, and reconciles us fully with the Father.

We are like shining stars in the dark of night, reflecting the Light of the world through our surrendered lives. Let's not be swayed by whispers of better things in the shadows; God is the goodness we long for. He is the fullness of our longings and the satisfaction we seek. Let us trust his will and his ways, aligning our lives in his love.

Listen for where love is directing you today and follow Jesus there.

It Will Be Clear

"Nothing is hidden that will not be made manifest,
nor is anything secret that will not be known
and come to light."

LUKE 8:17 ESV

Nothing done in secret will remain a secret forever.
Dark deeds committed with deceit and pride will not go
unnoticed. God will hold us to account, and he will not
let the shadows conceal what he sees clearly. But do not
despair in your commitment to integrity. Do not give up
doing the right thing in love, though others may not take
notice. God does. He sees, he knows, and he will not let it
go to waste.

When you are presented with the opportunity to take the
easy way out, urged that no one will know any different,
consider that God still sees. He still knows. Don't be tricked
into thinking that little lies don't mean a thing. Live your life
with honesty and continue to follow the leading of the Lord.
Integrity is worth the sacrifice of momentary ease. Live for
the audience of the Lord, for he doesn't miss a thing.

Choose to do the right thing even if no one is watching.

Help for Today

The Spirit also helps our weakness; for we do not
know how to pray as we should, but the Spirit Himself
intercedes for us with groanings too deep for words.

ROMANS 8:26 NASB

The Spirit is our help in every moment. The fellowship we
have with the Lord is uninterrupted and unhindered. Let us
not rely on our own waning strength when we have access
to the great grace of God through his Spirit.

Even when we do not know how to pray, the Spirit
intercedes for us. There is nothing that we are alone in.
There is no striving that we need do in any area of our
lives. Let's lean into the overwhelming goodness of our
constant companion and help today. Let's depend on him
in our joys and in our disappointments. God is our source.
He is the source of everything we need. Let's come to him
with open hearts, open minds, and yielded lives. Here is
where we find our overcoming strength.

Lean into the Spirit in prayer today.

Uncontainable

"Will God indeed dwell on the earth? Behold, heaven
and the highest heaven cannot contain You,
how much less this house which I have built!"

1 KINGS 8:27 NASB

When we try to fit God into our understanding, we
diminish his greatness and power. There is nothing that he
cannot do. The earth cannot contain him, nor can the vast
expanse of space. He is grander than our capacity to grasp.
He is more wonderful than we can dream. Instead of trying
to fit him in our mold, may we allow his love to broaden
our perspective in the great mystery of his enormity.

God is both greater than we can know and nearer than
we realize. He is not bound by flesh and bones. He is
the Spirit, and the Spirit goes wherever, however, and in
whatever measure he sees fit. There are no bounds to the
possibilities in his being. Let us give ourselves to knowing
his character, to knowing what he is truly like. Then we will
be able to recognize him in both the diamond and the dirt.

Acknowledge that God is greater than your circumstances.

Woven into Purpose

We are convinced that every detail of our lives is continually woven together to fit into God's perfect plan of bringing good into our lives, for we are his lovers who have been called to fulfill his designed purpose.

ROMANS 8:28 TPT

Do you trust that God can use seemingly meaningless things for his purposes? Do you look at the details of your life and wonder if they matter? Are you curious about how the random parts of your story will weave together into the tapestry of God's merciful plans? Whether or not you see intention in the small parts of your life, know that God does not miss a detail. When you recognize how he is weaving his love through the details of your story, you will marvel at his goodness.

Even the rubble and ashes of disappointed dreams will breed new life. He doesn't let darkness or destruction have the final word. He restores our hope; he redeems our broken dreams. He is at work even when we cannot sense it.

Trust that God will use every detail of your life for your good and for his glory.

Unmatched

What should we say then?
Since God is on our side,
who can be against us?

Romans 8:31 ncv

God is on the side of the vulnerable, and he is the defender of the weak. Let's be sure where we stand today. Are we living in his love, dedicated to seeing the abandoned cared for and the lonely put in families? We cannot solve all the world's problems, and it's not our job to do so. But we can display the lavish love of our Father by treating others the way that he treats us.

No one can stand against the Word of the Lord and win. He is victorious over all other powers. His love sets wrong things right. It breaks the power of sin cycles and the curse of death. We have been called in by the kindness of God, and we are called to stand out as living expressions of his kind care. May we cling to his faithfulness, following his path of peace, and promote his glorious goodness to all who will hear.

Rest in the confidence of God's faithfulness today.

Good Father

God has proved his love by giving us his greatest
treasure, the gift of his Son. And since God freely
offered him up as the sacrifice for us all, he certainly
won't withhold from us anything else he has to give.

ROMANS 8:32 TPT

There is nothing that God withholds from us. He did not
even keep his Son to himself; he sent him so that we would
know the extent of his compassion. Jesus freely laid down
his life so that we could clearly see the love that the Father
has. Nothing can compare to the merciful heart of God! No
grand gesture has ever been more pure or powerful.

God is as generous today as he was when he first sent
Jesus to us. He is abundant in kindness, welcoming us as
we turn to him. He took our shame, the weight of our sin,
and bore it himself so that we could be free from it. There
is now nothing that separates us from God. Not even the
strongest wall can keep us from his love. So, let us ask for
all that he has to offer. He is better than we could ever give
him credit for being.

*Ask what the Lord has for you today and receive it
with an open heart.*

Liberated

*"If the Son sets you free,
you are truly free."*

JOHN 8:36 NLT

The law of love does not require perfection from us. It is not a stringent standard that can easily interrupt our fellowship with God. We have been welcomed into the great expanse of God's kingdom by his mercy. The banner over our lives is love, and it is powerful enough to break the competing stories of shame that would keep us stuck in cycles of limited movement. Christ is our barrier-breaker! He has demolished the walls that kept us from moving freely in his compassion.

When we put parameters on our freedom, it suddenly ceases to be liberty at all. Christ came to set us free from the bondage of fear. He released us from the power of sin that would control us. We are free to live, to move, and to have our being. We are permitted to choose what we will! Let us only choose to never be enslaved by any other thing.

*Meditate on your freedom in Christ.
Make your choices today as one who is truly free.*

Declare His Goodness

"Return to your home, and declare how much God has done for you." So he went away, proclaiming throughout the city how much Jesus had done for him.

LUKE 8:39 NRSV

When we declare what God has done for us, we not only remind ourselves of his goodness, but we also invite others into it. Our testimony becomes the invitation for others to experience the same. God's work in our lives is not isolated. He longs for everyone to recognize the power of his love in their own stories.

May we take the words of Jesus seriously, knowing that he has intention behind everything he says. We are meant to share our lives with those around us. That includes sharing the good news of Jesus. When God's mercy meets us in tangible ways, let's not keep it to ourselves. We were made to share in our victories and to encourage one another in faith. How can you declare God's goodness today?

Share what God has done for you with others.

Wonderful Leader

"A child has been born to us; God has given a son to us. He will be responsible for leading the people. His name will be Wonderful Counselor, Powerful God, Father Who Lives Forever, Prince of Peace."

ISAIAH 9:6 NCV

Jesus is the best leader. He is full of wisdom, peace, and love. He is the wisest counselor we will ever know. He is the most powerful force in the universe. He is the bodily expression of the eternal Father. He is the Prince of peace. There is no shortage of mercy in his heart. Nothing is impossible for him.

Do you trust God to guide you in his goodness? Have you known his faithfulness toward you? He is loyal to his Word, and he is still speaking today. What does your relationship with the Lord look like? May you know the confidence of his presence through his Spirit with you. He gives revelation to expand your understanding of his kingdom. He speaks in simple and profound truth. Spend time in his Word and ask him to reveal greater depths of understanding within you.

Submit to Jesus' leadership today,
trusting his goodness to guide you.

Joy in His Presence

How happy your people must be!
How happy your officials,
who continually stand before you
and hear your wisdom!

2 CHRONICLES 9:7 NIV

The wisdom of God is not somber or overly serious. It causes joy because the truth of God's goodness sets us free! Even when he corrects us with his truth, our hearts come more alive in his love. He is not harsh with us, and his standards are not impossible to meet. What he wants from us is our trust, our submission, and our fellowship. He is so much better than we have yet experienced, so let's learn what he is like even more than what he does.

There is gladness in the presence of the Lord—overwhelming gladness! Those who continually fill up on the wisdom of God through fellowship with him know the deep, abiding joy of his nature. He is full of loyal and lavish love; he has all the answers we are looking for. He is full of power, and he moves in miracles of mercy. May we listen to his wisdom today and find the refreshing river of his delight.

Read through a chapter of Proverbs today.

Cheerful Giving

Let giving flow from your heart, not from a sense of religious duty. Let it spring up freely from the joy of giving—all because God loves hilarious generosity!

2 CORINTHIANS 9:7 TPT

God is not looking for our acts of obligation. He does not delight in our despairing obedience. We are not enslaved! We are children of the Most High, and we have freedom to choose how we will live and how we will give. Certainly, we cannot escape the responsibilities of life. There are some commitments that we should not grow lax in no matter how we feel about them.

When it comes to giving, God has offered us freedom to choose how we will do it. He loves a cheerful giver. When we take ownership of our rights to bless others, there is a partnership, not only in his love but also in his joy. Consider how you can lovingly reach out with tangible acts of kindness today. Decide what you can give and what you want to give. Ask the Lord for his input, and you may be surprised at his suggestions. Whatever you choose, give it with joy and anticipation. You are in charge of how you will contribute, so do it with intention.

Decide in your heart to intentionally give today and follow through on it.

Increase

This generous God who supplies abundant seed for the farmer, which becomes bread for our meals, is even more extravagant toward you. First he supplies every need, plus more. Then he multiplies the seed as you sow it, so that the harvest of your generosity will grow.

2 CORINTHIANS 9:10 TPT

Have you considered lately that what you have, God had a hand in providing? He gives seed for the person who plants. He makes sure the hungry have something to eat. As we work with what we have, God blesses it. Everything that we do with diligence will reap a reward. Nothing goes to waste in his kingdom.

Have you grown weary of persevering in certain areas of your life? Ask God for his perspective today. Ask him for wisdom to keep pressing in where it is important and wisdom to know when to back off in pursuits that don't serve you well. It is never too late to redirect. The Lord is your help and your strength, and he will increase the return. Don't grow weary in doing good in the name of love, for he will take your offerings and add his own abundance to it.

Put your hand to the work you have to do
and thank God for blessing it.

Restoration Is Coming

Return to the stronghold, you prisoners of hope.
Even today I declare that I will restore double to you.

ZECHARIAH 9:12 NKJV

Is there an area of your life that has been stripped down? Do you feel something has been robbed from you? What areas of struggle have you wondering about the future? Turn to Jesus and receive from the overflow of his love. There is more than enough to encourage, strengthen, and refresh you. Take heart and take hope today, for God is our restorer.

Where hope has waned, look to the Lord. With God, all things are possible. His solutions are better than any we could come up with on our own. He is not worried about your future. He is able to do far more than you could ask him. He is not fearful for you. Rest in the confidence of his faithfulness as he turns the rubble of our disappointment into fields of glory. There is so much life that is coming! This is not the end for you. Hear his declaration over you that breakthrough is ahead.

Turn to God in hope for a breakthrough.

July

I will thank the LORD
because he is just;
I will sing praise
to the name of the LORD Most High.

PSALM 7:17 NLT

Mercy over Sacrifice

"Now you should go and study the meaning of the verse: I want you to show mercy, not just offer me a sacrifice. For I have come to invite the outcasts of society and sinners, not those who think they are already on the right path."

MATTHEW 9:13 TPT

There is beauty in sacrifice. There is worth in our giving. Let's remember, though, that mercy cannot be an afterthought. Mercy is what moves the heart of God. Everything God does is motivated by love. May we let compassion also move us out of our comfort zones.

Imagine seeing someone begging for bread, their hunger apparent. Now imagine telling that person that you will pay to plant a tree in their name. Is it sacrifice? Perhaps. Is it mercy? Not even close. A merciful act would be to feed them. Mercy meets people where they are and addresses their needs. There are no varying levels of compassion. Every bit counts—even the smallest act. Let love lead you outside of your ideas of what giving should look like. Don't judge a person's worth based on their outer appearance.

Offer kindness to someone in need today.

Faithful Mercy

It depends not on human will or exertion,
but on God, who has mercy.

ROMANS 9:16 ESV

God takes our meager efforts in love and goes far above and beyond what we could ever do. That is good news! Let's not run ourselves into the ground, thinking that the more we do, the more we will receive. God is faithful in kindness, and he will follow through on every one of his promises, no matter our response. This is not an excuse to blow off our responsibilities, either. This is an invitation to partner with God in all that we do and trust that God will cover all that we miss.

Burnout is not godly. Exhaustion is not a marker of our worth. May we learn to rest in the confidence of God's faithfulness. He is able to do far more than we could imagine doing. He delights in giving us his strength in our weakness. He loves to help us. Let's lean on him rather than pushing ourselves beyond the brink. His love is strong.

Instead of trying harder today, trust that God is bigger
than your abilities and rely on his mercy.

Help Me

Immediately the boy's father exclaimed, "I do believe;
help me overcome my unbelief!"

MARK 9:24 NIV

When God speaks to us, he does so in truth and in love.
Though we may believe him, we may also recognize parts
of our hearts that are not quite convinced. It is okay to
respond to God with, "I do believe; help me overcome my
unbelief!" The tension of the two can coexist within us—
simultaneous belief and doubt.

Instead of belittling ourselves in our lack of understanding,
may we ask God for help. Instead of trying harder to
believe and spiritually bypassing the parts of us that need
help in trusting God, let's turn to him for assurance. Our
faith comes from him; he is the source of it all. We have no
ability to believe without him. So, let us come to him with
the reality of our struggle. He will not demean us or turn us
away. How incredible it is that, even in our very belief, God
is the one who mercifully gives out of the abundance of
who he is.

Ask God for help in believing his truth.

Training Ground

Everyone who competes in the games goes into strict training. They do it to get a crown that will not last, but we do it to get a crown that will last forever.

1 CORINTHIANS 9:25 NIV

Have you ever trained for a competition? Perhaps you were going to run a marathon. Maybe it was a musical program. Think over a time when you directed your focus into an event and consider the amount of discipline and intentionality it took.

If we spend time disciplining our minds and bodies for a goal, how much more should we train our spirits? Living with intention, being cognizant of how we use our time and the things we put our attention to, requires mindfulness. May we be people of integrity who use our freedom in Christ to transform into his loving image. Wherever this finds you today, this is your training ground. It's time to take charge and press into the transformative process of focused growth.

Make a list of three things you can do this week to train your spirit.

Gracious God

In Your great mercy You did not
utterly consume them nor forsake them;
For You are God, gracious and merciful.

NEHEMIAH 9:31 NKJV

Though God is able to both create and destroy, his mercy
moves him to be patient with us. He is slow to anger, long-
lasting in hopeful help, and he is strong to save us from
every pit and peril. He does not leave us to waste away in
our sin, not even when we choose it. He is always close,
always willing to help us, and he is full of love that washes
us clean of every prideful choice.

May we be gracious as God is gracious. May we look for
ways to extend mercy to others even when they are in
situations of their own making. We are constantly being
reached by love, so let's constantly reach out to others
with the same compassion. We have been delivered from
much, and so can others who are struggling in detrimental
cycles. God is near to all who call on his name. He never
abandons us! May we look like him in our surrendered lives.

Reach out to a friend and encourage them.

His Choice

"No one takes it from me, but I lay it down of my own accord. I have authority to lay it down, and I have authority to take it up again. This charge I have received from my Father."

JOHN 10:8 ESV

Life does not simply happen to us. In any moment, we are able to choose how we will respond. We get to choose the mindsets that we live by. God is faithful to save. He is long-lasting in loyal love. Jesus, when coming to this earth, chose to live out the Father's love. He chose to partner with mercy and show us the way to the kingdom of God.

Though we cannot control what will happen in this life, we do get to choose our reactions and responses. We get to take ownership of the attitude of our hearts. We get to choose who we turn to for help when we need it. Will we live with the foundation of our faith in Jesus? Will we trust him to do what we cannot? Will we rely on his faithfulness more than our own? He is good. He is better than any other. Whatever we choose, let's own it today.

Take ownership of your choices today while knowing that the posture of your heart matters.

Fearless Confidence

The one who walks in integrity
will experience a fearless confidence in life,
but the one who is devious
will eventually be exposed.

PROVERBS 10:9 TPT

When we live with integrity, there is no need to fear being found out. When we are honest about ourselves and our intentions and when we make choices in line with love, there is nothing to hide. Fearless confidence accompanies those who live without deception. Though we are not perfect, there is grace to cover our weaknesses.

Have you ever felt like you needed to hide something about yourself in order to be accepted? The Lord welcomes you with open arms, and he sees your heart clearly. Feeling inadequate is not the same as being devious. Know that love will not expose your fears. Love relieves them! The Father is full of mercy. May you live with honesty and transparency before the Lord and others. You are fully known and fully loved.

Be true to your word and follow through on something you have been putting off.

Holy Endurance

No temptation has overtaken you but such as is
common to man; and God is faithful, who will not allow
you to be tempted beyond what you are able, but with
the temptation will provide the way of escape also, so
that you will be able to endure it.

1 Corinthians 10:13 NASB

Not every opportunity in this life is a welcome one. We
need wisdom from the Lord to help us discern what is for
our benefit and what will lead us away from love. There are
countless temptations that we will face in this life. Most of
them require bypassing what we know to be true. Little
compromises add up to bigger ones along the way.

Today, when you are faced with temptation, look to Jesus.
He knows what it is like to be tempted. Do you forget that
he also faced the weakness of humanity? Let him help you
with his sufficient grace. Let him speak his truth and wisdom
to your heart. You are not isolated in your struggle; he is
with you. The God of the ages is your strength and your
help! He will give you the ability to endure what you could
not on your own. He is your breakthrough, so look to him.

*Look to Jesus for help in overcoming invitations
that do not align with your values or his kingdom.*

Whatever You Do

Whether you eat or drink,
or whatever you do,
do all to the glory of God.

1 Corinthians 10:31 NKJV

There will be times when we have to do the things we don't want to do. Menial responsibilities don't become obsolete in our walk with the Lord. Not everything is fun, and that is okay. The joy of the Lord is found not in what we do, but in who is with us through it all. We can pay our bills, wash the dishes, and take out the trash, all the while glorifying God.

When we reduce our purpose to mountaintop moments of victory, we overlook the power we have in our daily choices. Taking the dog for a walk can be just as meaningful as connecting with a friend. No matter what we do, we can do it with our hearts postured in humble love before the Father. When we do it for the Lord, knowing he is with us in it, everything becomes worship.

Worship God with your choices today.

Easy to Find

"Everyone who asks will receive.
The one who searches will find.
And everyone who knocks
will have the door opened."

LUKE 11:10 NCV

God is accessible, and he is near to those who call on him.
Whatever you need, ask your Father. He hears you, and
he will answer you. Jesus made this clear by saying that
"everyone who asks will receive." Look for the Lord, and
you will find him. Ask him for help, and you will have it.

What feels out of reach today? Is there a problem that you
just can't seem to solve, a person that you are struggling
to reconcile with, or a task that you have been putting
off doing? Whatever it is that you lack, God has it in
abundance. He will strengthen you with his grace. He
will encourage you in his love. He will instruct you in his
wisdom. He brings clarity to confusion, and he makes rocky
paths smooth. Don't hesitate to ask him for what you need.
Press into his presence.

Ask the Lord for more of his wisdom today.

Healed Hearts

"I will give them one heart, and put a new spirit within them. And I will take the heart of stone out of their flesh and give them a heart of flesh."

EZEKIEL 11:19 NASB

Have you ever felt so jaded by the world that you could sense a wall around your heart, keeping you from engaging with others in love? We all have wounds from our past, from childhood to recent events. No family system is perfect, and we learn to cope in the best ways we know. For some, this looks like shutting out pain and staying away from those who would manipulate them. For others, this could mean overextending themselves in an effort to help the people around them, all the while feeling resentful for the lack of reciprocation.

Whatever story your past holds, know that the Lord is your healer. He is the one who mends broken hearts. Will you allow him access to your heart? Will you let his love wash over you, even if the feelings you encounter are uncomfortable at first? In healing, there is a process. But the Lord knows what he is doing. You weren't meant to push away emotions. You are meant to know God in them.

Thank God for his Spirit that heals your heart and connects you to his own.

It Is Yours

"I tell you, whatever you ask in prayer,
believe that you have received it,
and it will be yours."

MARK 11:24 ESV

A promise is only as good as the one who delivers them. If we are accustomed to empty pledges from people who do not follow through on their word, it may take us time to learn to trust a reliable source. It is okay if this is a process! It is bound to be. Let us continue to press into knowing the Lord and his nature. What is he like? Is he trustworthy?

In the process of growing our trust, we need to test the waters of faith. We will not grow unless we take steps to do so. Today, let's ask the Lord for something specific. Let's lift our prayers to him, connecting to his Spirit and asking for revelation of his goodness. Let's stretch the parameters of our belief by going further than we have before in asking for what we need. He is good, he is faithful, and he will always follow through.

Ask, pray, and believe that the Lord will answer you.

Blessed Obedience

"Blessed rather are those
who hear the word of God
and obey it."

LUKE 11:28 NIV

Faith without follow-through is not faith at all. What we truly believe, we will live out. May we align our lives with the kingdom of heaven, following the instructions that Jesus has given us. There is so much practical advice within God's Word. There are the core values of his kingdom deposited throughout the Scriptures, and there are also clear examples on how to live them.

Instead of making excuses for why we are not obeying the voice of the Lord, let's commit to putting his Word into practice. We can hear things all day long, but listening requires a response. What will our response to the Word of the Lord be? What a beautiful gift it is that he speaks to us through Scriptures and through his Spirit. What a wonderful reality it is to walk with him in living relationship.

Respond to God's Word with your actions today.

Refreshed by Love

"Simply join your life with mine. Learn my ways and you'll discover that I'm gentle, humble, easy to please. You will find refreshment and rest in me."

MATTHEW 11:29 TPT

There is nothing more refreshing than being reminded of someone's love for us. The pure, powerful love of God is always available, always overflowing, and full of all the goodness we are looking for. The love of God covers us in our weakness, lifts us up in our discouragement, and speaks life over the seeds that have been planted in our lives.

Walking with the Lord is not complicated. Simply join your life to his; let him have access to your heart. Give him your attention. Submit to his mercy. Learn what he is like, and you will find that he is full of patience and kindness, and he is so very easy to please. May you find the rest that your soul needs in his presence today. His desire is for you to know him as deeply as you are known by him.

Spend time in the presence of God listening for his voice and waiting on his peace.

Fearless Trust

Behold, God is my salvation,
I will trust and not be afraid;
For the Lord God is my strength and my song,
And He has become my salvation.

Isaiah 12:2 nasb

When we experience fear, our nervous systems react in visceral ways. We may all of a sudden feel frozen. We may run from the threat we feel, or we may fight against the fear that presents itself. In the perfect love of God, fear has no power. Jesus has overcome every potential terror with the strength of his constant mercy.

Instead of letting fear overtake us when we experience the familiar feelings of anxiety, let's turn to the Lord in the moment. As we give him our attention and remind ourselves that we are safe in him, we make room for the peace of God to flood our minds. We can practice putting our trust in him over and over again. As we do, it will become a more natural reaction. No matter what, God is our salvation. He is our help, our strength, and our song. He is trustworthy!

When you experience fear or worry today,
wait on the Lord. Put your trust in him.

Transformed Thoughts

Don't copy the behavior and customs of this world, but let God transform you into a new person by changing the way you think. Then you will learn to know God's will for you, which is good and pleasing and perfect.

ROMANS 12:2 NLT

How we think is not set in stone. Just because we've believed something to be true does not mean that we cannot change our minds when presented with better information. In relationship with God, as he instructs us in his wisdom and reveals aspects of his kingdom truths, our understanding broadens. May we never be so stuck in the mindsets that we have taken for granted that we are not willing to grow in our perception of mercy.

We should be aware that just because we are taught something in the church doesn't make it biblical. Let's be wise and discerning. The Lord does not drive divisions; he brings us together in unity. He encourages mercy, not judgment. He is full of compassion, and his requirements are not empty. As our knowledge of God grows, so will our thoughts transform to be more like his.

Spend time in God's Word and ask for revelation to know his kingdom thoughts.

Drink Deeply

With joy you will drink deeply
from the fountain of salvation!

ISAIAH 12:3 NLT

There is joy in the salvation of the Lord. There is hope in his promises. There is peace in his presence. There is abundantly more than we could ever need. His love does not run out, and his power does not run dry. There is always more than enough. Let us leave behind our scarcity mindsets and drink deeply from the bottomless well of Christ's mercy.

When was the last time you felt joy at the thought of knowing God? When did you last celebrate being found in him? May you take the opportunity that today has brought you to remember the gratitude, peace, and pure delight you felt in the beginning. Remember the freedom that you have been given, the overcoming strength you have access to. May the flame of your joy burn brightly, and may the living waters of God's mercy refresh, restore, and rejuvenate your soul.

Thank God for the gift of his salvation.

Sing a New Song

Praise the LORD in song,
for He has done excellent things;
let this be known throughout the earth.

ISAIAH 12:5 NASB

Singing can be a fantastic way to shift our perspective. Sometimes, when we feel stuck in a negative emotional space, singing can help us release that feeling. It gets our souls moving. Let's not dismiss the importance of expression through music. It is liberating and reflective, and it is a beautiful practice. Our emotions can connect to melodies, so let's use them!

Think about how the Lord has moved in your life. Consider a time when you could sense his nearness and his overwhelming goodness. Sing from that place. Sing from gratitude from that moment. As your heart begins to shift, sing too from the reality of your current circumstances. Rise above the struggle and sing to the Lord a new song. Let your voice ring out, no matter how it sounds. The Lord loves to hear you!

Sing a song of gratitude to the Lord today,
recognizing his goodness toward you.

Same God

God works in different ways, but it is the same God who does the work in all of us.

1 CORINTHIANS 12:6 NLT

The Lord is the same God he has always been, so much greater than our humanity and our understanding. He cannot be relegated to the categories we use for each other. He extends beyond them all. What is created cannot contain the Creator. He is more than the sum of all things.

When we see differences in each other, they should excite us rather than discourage us. We are not created to be carbon copies of one another. The diversity of creation reveals the creativity of our God. May we learn to celebrate the unique expressions of divine love in each other's lives! God works in a wonderful variety of ways, so let's not make him smaller in our minds than he is. Let's dare expand our understanding as we continually discover how vast he is. His nature remains the same, no matter how differently he moves.

Look for the fruit of the Spirit in others' lives rather than looking at outward appearances.

Not One Forgotten

"Are not five sparrows sold for two cents?
Yet not one of them is forgotten before God."

Luke 12:6 NASB

What seems meaningless to us is not meaningless to God.
Though we overlook many things, God does not miss any of
it. After the rain, when worms are flooded from their homes,
we may not pay them attention, but God does. Nothing is
so insignificant that God does not pay attention to it.

May we become more aware of how involved God is in
the little things of life. As we find him there, we will be
encouraged in knowing that he really is in all things. Our
faith will grow as our understanding swells to include his
loving care and consideration over every detail of our lives.
There is nothing that escapes his notice. How wonderful is
his attention to detail! How great is his memory! May we be
encouraged that he will not forget what he has promised
to do. He is faithful.

Take time to notice little things today.

Common Good

To each is given the manifestation of the Spirit for the common good.

1 CORINTHIANS 12:7 ESV

God has not overlooked you. He has not withheld his Spirit from some and given him freely to others. We all receive from the same abundance, the same power, and the same merciful heart. It simply looks different in each of our lives. We do not all have the same abilities. We don't all share the same passions in life. We are, however, given the same values to live by. Love's call beckons each of us with the same intensity and purpose.

Whatever gifts you have, whatever talents you possess, may you use them with others in mind. With love as your motivation, everything you do has impact. May you harness the power of your choices by joining your heart with the Lord's compassion and looking for ways to serve others with your gifts. Ask the Spirit for ideas today, and may you partner with him in testing them out.

Serve the greater good with your gifts today.

Just Grace

Each time he said, "My grace is all you need. My power works best in weakness." So now I am glad to boast about my weaknesses, so that the power of Christ can work through me.

2 Corinthians 12:9 NLT

How do you feel when you are on a roll, full of energy and motivation? You may feel capable and unstoppable. You may not even think about how you feel, instead just moving from one thing to the next with ease. What a wonderful sensation that is! Though these days, weeks, and seasons are a delight to experience, they do not make us more or less worthy than any other time.

Jesus is as sure about his love for you in your weakness as he is in your strength. He takes delight in you, no matter the state of your confidence. When you are weak, it is an opportunity to know the great grace of God in powerful ways. As Paul reminds us, God's power works best in weakness. Even your limitations are something to be grateful for.

Thank God for your weakness today, recognizing there is more room for his grace to work.

Part of a Whole

The body does not consist of one member but of many.

1 CORINTHIANS 12:14 ESV

We each are unique reflections of God's image. He does not make duplicates, expecting us all to look the same. His vast nature is displayed in the diversity of the universe. He is endlessly creative, and that applies as much to us as it does to flora and fauna. We were each thoughtfully and wonderfully made.

Have you been striving to become like others, denying parts of yourself in the process? God wants your freedom. You are not meant to conform to the patterns of this world, and that includes blending into systems, communities, and friend groups where you have to hide who you are. Ask God today who he says you are. Ask him for his perspective on your life. Will you love yourself and then allow others to freely be themselves, too?

Do not compare your life to others; recognize that you are unique and have something wonderful to offer others.

Stay the Course

Do not turn aside; for then you would go after
empty things which cannot profit or deliver,
for they are nothing.

1 SAMUEL 12:21 NKJV

What are the driving forces of your life? What are you
working toward? Having goals in life is important; living
with vision is imperative. The Word of God says that
"without vision, the people perish (Proverbs 29:18)." Let us
consider what vision keeps us moving forward.

If you feel a little lost at sea in this season of your life,
having no clear vision for the future, you can still rest in the
presence of Jesus with you. Whether you are simply trying
to get through the day or you are living in the fruit of your
dreams, know that relationship with the Lord is yours. He is
as full of love for you in your breakthrough as he is in your
heartbreak. Look to him, fix your eyes on Jesus, and let him
be your vision when you have nothing else.

Keep turning your thoughts to Jesus throughout your day.

People of God

The LORD will not abandon His people on account of His great name, because the LORD has been pleased to make you a people for Himself.

1 SAMUEL 12:22 NASB

The Lord promises to never abandon his people. He vows to always be with us. His kingdom is inclusive, and he welcomes all with the same great, powerful love. It is his delight to make us a people for himself. Jesus made it clear that the Father feels as much compassion for those who have never heard his name as the Israelites who worshiped him throughout their history. He draws us in with kindness, and he calls us his own.

Have you submitted your life to the love of Jesus? Then you are his! Have you known the power of his persistent presence? He is close to the broken-hearted, and he is near to those who rejoice in celebration. His freedom is for all who come to him. He sets the captives free, and he makes the disheartened dance with the joy of their liberty. What a wonderful kingdom we have been ushered into. There is more to discover in his great love!

Recognize that the family of God is diverse and look for beauty in the differences.

All Your Heart

"Only fear the LORD and serve him faithfully
with all your heart. For consider what great things
he has done for you."

1 SAMUEL 12:24 ESV

Where your heart is, there will be your treasure. Jesus'
words resound with truth. They are as applicable today as
they were when he first spoke them. When we give God
access to our whole hearts, leaning into the fellowship we
have with his Spirit through Christ, we are transformed by
his living love.

What does it look like to fear the Lord? Does it mean that
we cower before him and fear his retribution? Or does it
mean that we honor his unmatched wisdom, leading, and
love? When we submit our lives to the Lord, we give him
the right to lead us. Perfect love casts out fear. It offers us
freedom. When we get to know the beautiful and merciful
nature of God, we cannot help but to love him. Why would
we strike out on our own when companionship with the
Creator of all things is ours? What great things he does for
us! What abundant mercy he shows us.

*Consider how good God has been to you
and give him access to your whole heart.*

Rediscover Wonder

Since we are receiving a kingdom that cannot be shaken, let us be thankful, and so worship God acceptably with reverence and awe.

HEBREWS 12:28 NIV

Though power dynamics in this world rise and fall with the shifting of regimes, political parties, and the wealthy, the kingdom of God is unshakable. When we partner with God in prayer and in our lifestyles of compassion in action, we invite heaven to invade earth through the coming of his kingdom.

Jesus performed miracles of mercy that changed people's lives forever. He promised that we would do the same, and even greater. Are we living in the power of his presence? Are we praying for the greater things of his kingdom to manifest in our lives and in this world? Let's not grow weary in uniting with the Lord in his purposes. He knows best, and we can trust his wisdom. Jesus will one day return with the fullness of his glorious victory. Let's not lose sight of his coming!

Meditate on the coming kingdom of God and thank him for his perfect wisdom.

Trust Him

> "Do not keep striving for what you are to eat and what you are to drink, and do not keep worrying."
>
> LUKE 12:29 NRSV

Have you ever considered where the worries you have about provision come from? Perhaps you were raised in a home where money was tight. Maybe you knew what it was like to not know where your next meal would come from. Perhaps you have always had enough, and worry seems to infiltrate your mind without an obvious history of lack.

God is our good, good Father. He does not offer his children stones when they ask for bread. He does not trick them by offering one thing and switching it out at the last moment. He is honest, he is kind, and he is transparent. He is abundant, full of all that we need. He will take care of us. Let's trust him to do it! And when we struggle to trust, let's ask for his help. Don't hesitate to look for encouragement in trusted friends and fellow lovers of God. What God has done for others, he will also do for us. Though it may look different, his faithful nature will never fail, and he will provide.

*Stop striving for simple necessities
and give God your worries.*

Cared For

"People everywhere seem to worry about making a living, but your heavenly Father knows your every need and will take care of you."

LUKE 12:30 TPT

Lay aside your worries today. Lay down thoughts of how you will get from where you are to where you need to be. God is faithful, and this is true in every question and in every solution. He is a faithful leader, a constant help, our consistent strength, and the one who works all things together for our good. Where you cannot see a way out, look to Jesus. Where you cannot see a path forward, fix your attention on where God is.

We cannot exaggerate the love of God. We can't overstate his goodness. He is infinitely better than we could ever describe. He has more abundance in him then we can fathom. He really is good. He really is for us. He really does care for us more than our mothers, fathers, closest friends, and advocates. Let's turn our thoughts to him even now, inviting the peace of his presence to lead us into rest. As he meets us, we will grow in deeper confidence and trust.

Rest in the tender and confident care of your Father.

Godly Longings

Earnestly desire the greater gifts.
And I show you a still more excellent way.

1 CORINTHIANS 12:31 NASB

God gives freely to all who ask. Though we are born with certain leanings and talents that come naturally, we can grow in areas that don't come easily with determination, focus, and consistency. When we earnestly desire something, our actions propel us in our motivations. May we press into those areas, and may we practice endurance and patience, putting the work in.

When was the last time you felt longing in your heart for the Lord? Can you recall when you hungered and thirsted for more of his power in your life? There are seasons when our growth dictates our hunger, and there are times that our desires affect our growth. Today is a fresh opportunity to press into the presence of the Lord. He is near, and he is full of all that we could ever long for.

Let the desire for more of God's power in your life lead you to ask him for greater gifts.

Humble Love

Love is patient and kind.
Love is not jealous or boastful or proud.

1 CORINTHIANS 13:4 NLT

The love of God is humble. It does not seek to be right. It does not put down others in order to be lifted up. It is not in a rush. It is overflowing, and it is always kind. It reaches us in the reality of our present moment, not in the fantasy of the future. It uplifts the lowly and heals the broken. It is powerful, it is restorative, and it is full of hope.

What kind of love do you live by? Is compassion evident in your life? Are you patient with others and humble in your exchanges with them? Today, look to Jesus to see what laid-down love resembles. Love is not hasty, and it is not anxious. It is full of peace, confidence, and trust. May you find the endless source of Jesus' love as your foundation for every relationship and interaction.

*Choose to be patient with others today,
knowing that God is patient with you.*

August

**Thanks be to God
for his indescribable gift!**

2 CORINTHIANS 9:15 NRSV

Follow Him

You shall follow the LORD your God and fear Him;
and you shall keep His commandments,
listen to His voice, serve Him, and cling to Him.

DEUTERONOMY 13:4 NASB

What does it look like to follow God? Is it not to listen to his voice, serve him, and cling to him? This sounds so simple! And yet, it takes intention and consistency to grow in our relationship with the Lord. He is always pursuing us in love. He is full of wisdom to instruct us in the best way to live.

Do you make it a practice to listen to the Lord's voice throughout your day? The Holy Spirit is your constant companion and help. He is always speaking. Listening is a skill you can grow in. Start with the revelation of his nature through his Word. Let the Scriptures instruct your knowledge of how he moves. Listen for his loving and powerful truths. As you keep an open line of communication throughout your day, you will find that he is more involved than you could imagine in the details of your life.

*When you feel judgment rising,
try to consider the other person's point of view.*

No Record

[Love] keeps no record of wrongs.

1 CORINTHIANS 13:5 NIV

Love does not keep a record of hurts. It does not store up a memory of wrongs. Thank God that when we ask for forgiveness, he gives it freely! When we repent, he does not hold our pasts against us. Though we may or may not be reconciled to those who have hurt us, we can let go of the weight of their wounds and choose to forgive them.

Forgiveness is as much for our sakes as it is for the offender. We do not need to condone another's behavior to forgive them for it. When we let go of the need for retaliation or even for their understanding, we free ourselves from expectations that may never be met. Let's trust God to handle our hearts. Let's trust him to heal our wounds. No one else can perfectly meet our expectations outside of him, but that does not mean that we don't know love in our lives. Let's practice his kingdom love, ripping up the records we have kept against others.

Let go of an offense today.

Contentment in Christ

Be content with what you have, because God has said,
"Never will I leave you;
never will I forsake you"

HEBREWS 13:5 NIV

When we practice contentment in our present circumstances, we train our minds to look for the good that is there. It may take some digging at first, but we can find goodness in every moment. We can begin with what is always true: God is with us. He will never leave us. He will never abandon us. What a beautiful gift we have in his presence in our lives! He is with us in the fog of uncertainty, and he is with us in the fields of harvest.

Here, in this moment, there is air to breathe. There is a shelter over our heads. There is sun to warm our skin. There are clothes to keep us protected from the elements. There is food for our bellies. There is refreshing water to quench our thirst. What is accessible to you right now that you might otherwise take for granted?

Write a list of what you are thankful for in this moment.

Hold On

Love never gives up, never loses faith, is always hopeful, and endures through every circumstance.

1 Corinthians 13:7 NLT

When you are tempted to give up, what can you do to turn that around? Sometimes, it's as simple as taking a break. We are not meant to work ourselves into the ground. Rest is holy! It is important to take time away. Other times, we need to focus on our nutrition. Have we eaten recently? Was it nourishing? Our bodies are not machines; what we put in them can affect the quality of our thoughts and attention.

Love takes care of itself. It is never depleted. Is your tank filled up today? Is it running low? If you are struggling to find hope, don't beat yourself up about it. Shaming yourself for your weakness will do nothing to help you turn that around. As you endure, you can find hope in the nearness of God. When you don't know what else to do, look to him. He is full of wisdom, discernment, and love to fill you up.

Look for the bright side today.

Reliable Love

Love never fails.

1 CORINTHIANS 13:8 NCV

You have probably heard the saying, "love is the answer." Well, what is the question? you may wonder. Anything you could possibly imagine. There are no exceptions to this. What love looks like may be different than you expect, however. God's love is the strongest force in the universe, for it is his very nature. Love is not flimsy; it is strong. Love is not coddling. It is not the easy way out. It does not make excuses for other's poor behavior. It does not encourage abuse.

It takes humility to choose compassion when we would rather turn away in indifference. It takes self-control to choose mercy over retaliation. Though it is not easy, the mandate to love is simple. Let's stop complicating the law of love that Christ laid out by adding our own preferences to the mix. His love never fails. Choosing to love like him will lead us not into destruction but into the abundance of his life.

When you don't know how to respond, choose love.

Never Changes

Jesus Christ is the same yesterday
and today and forever.

HEBREWS 13:8 NASB

When we look at the life of Jesus as presented to us through the Scriptures, we can know that Jesus is the same today as he was then. His nature remains unchanged. Who he was in the beginning, he remains now.

When was the last time you acquainted yourself with Jesus in the Word? Have you spent time reading through the Gospels and discovering (or rediscovering) his compassion, his kindness, and his heart? There is so much for us to find in fellowship with his Spirit. The Spirit illuminates the Word and brings revelation to the deep truths of the kingdom of God. There is no mystery that he won't reveal. There is no problem too difficult for his wisdom. Spend some time looking at the life of Jesus, reading his words, and asking the Spirit to reveal his heart in even more depth.

Read a chapter in the Gospels today.

Keep Growing

When I was a child, I used to speak like a child, think like a child, reason like a child; when I became a man, I did away with childish things.

1 Corinthians 13:11 niv

Children can only understand so much. With limited experience in life, there is so much that they are continually taking in and learning through different developmental stages. They have great capacity for belief, and the wonder they feel when discovering something new is remarkable. They are tenacious and adaptable.

As we mature, we adapt our thinking to include a broader understanding of the world and its ways. A child may look at the moon and see a face, thinking a man lives there. As they grow and learn about the craters that become shadows as the sun reflects off the surface, they put away the fantastical thought of a personified moon. So, too, may we realize that some things we thought when we were young in our faith will change with our broadening understanding of God and his kingdom.

Recognize where your understanding needs to change.

Above All Else

Until then, there are three things that remain: faith, hope, and love—yet love surpasses them all. So above all else, let love be the beautiful prize for which you run.

1 CORINTHIANS 13:13 TPT

If you are tired of being reminded of the importance of love, perhaps what you need today is a fresh revelation of its power. There truly is nothing more indicative of God and his kingdom than the strength of his mercy. When it all boils down, what is left? Faith, hope, and love. How do these show up in your life?

In our interactions with others, are we considering ourselves as more important than they? Do we elevate our own comfort over kindness? Do we let our limited scope of understanding keep us from acting in compassion? Whatever we do, whether in word or in deed, may we do it with faith in God's faithfulness and hope in his promises with his love as our unshakable foundation and ultimate motivation.

Make love the goal of your interactions today.

Beautiful Fruit

By Him let us continually offer the sacrifice
of praise to God, that is, the fruit of our lips,
giving thanks to His name.

HEBREWS 13:15 NKJV

When we think about what we say, how we say it, and the fruit of our words, we offer God the sacrifice of our praise. This is a form of worship. When we take time to thank him, we are building a practice of gratitude that will transform our perspective. This, too, is worship. When we live with intention to know and serve God, he is pleased.

How can you honor the Lord with your words today? Take time to thank him out loud for the blessings you have. Look for ways to encourage others. Speak out the good you see in them. Look for opportunities to bring peace to situations. Reflect on what you want to be known of you and how you want others to feel around you. Where there is a disconnect between intention and action, implement the change you want to see. There are countless opportunities before you today to practice offering the Lord the fruit of your lips.

Think about what you say before you speak.

Confidence in Christ

"Don't worry or surrender to your fear. For you've believed in God, now trust and believe in me also."

JOHN 14:1 TPT

Jesus is the way, the truth, and the life. He is the peace in every storm. He is the loyal love that covers us at all times. He is our Savior, the one who broke the chains of our fear and shame. He is our liberator and our Redeemer. He is the one who was, who is, and who is to come. He is constant in mercy, consistent in grace, and full of unmatched power.

What has you worried today? What fears are keeping you from moving forward in peace? Give them to Jesus, for he is more than able to carry the weight of your cares. You are not alone in your struggles, and you are not isolated in your trouble. Jesus is with you. His Spirit is your source of strength, hope, and love. There is more than enough peace in his presence for you now and forever. Press in. Let him be your confidence!

Take Jesus at his Word and trust him with everything that threatens your peace in him.

Abundant Life

"I am the way, the truth, and the life.
No one can come to the Father except through me."

JOHN 14:6 NLT

Jesus paved the way to the Father for all to come through him. When we look at the Son, he is the living expression of the Father's love. There is nothing that the Father hides from the Son, so when we come through Jesus, we enter into the fullness of their fellowship. There is nothing that separates us from the love of God in Christ. There is no wall of hostility, no doubt that could interrupt the passion of his heart.

No matter what you are doing today, look to Jesus. Come to him now and fix your attention on his unchanging nature. He is full of loyal love toward you. He is wisdom incarnate. Everything you need is found in him. There is more goodness, more life, more hope, more joy, more peace, more kindness, more of every fruit of the Spirit—always more in his glorious presence.

Look to Jesus first and often as you go about your day.

Rebirth

There is hope for a tree, if it is cut down,
that it will sprout again,
and that its tender shoots will not cease.

JOB 14:7 NKJV

What tender hope we have in Christ. He is like a cool breeze on a hot day. He is like refreshing rains after a drought. He is the food that nourishes us when we are hungry. He is all that and so much more.

No matter what troubles you have faced, no matter the destruction you have experienced in your life, the Lord your God will redeem and restore you. He does not ignore your cries for help. He does not turn away from you in your grief. He speaks a better word over you. If there is hope for a tree to sprout again, how much more hope is there for you to experience renewal? Put your trust in him, for he is able to do far more than you can even imagine him doing.

Speak hope over any despair you feel.

Peace and Joy

The kingdom of God is not eating and drinking, but righteousness and peace and joy in the Holy Spirit.

ROMANS 14:17 NASB

For every trouble, there is an invitation for peace. For our grief and mourning, there is also joy coming. There is more available to us in the Spirit of God than we can know. He is full of abundance for every situation. Every moment is an opportunity to know the great grace of God.

The kingdom of God is not about what we wear, how we eat, or what jobs we have. It is not in which friend group we are a part of or what city we live in. It is not what nationality we are or what language we speak. The kingdom of God is in how the Spirit dwells and shows up in our lives. How? In the fruit of the Spirit we see poured out. Where there is righteousness, there is the kingdom. Where the peace of God is, there he dwells. Where there is deep, abiding joy in his presence, there is the fullness of God in us. May we humbly look for the fruit of his work in our lives, giving thanks every time we spot it.

Look for the fruit of the Spirit outside of rules and regulations today.

Helper

> "The Helper, the Holy Spirit, whom the Father will send in My name, He will teach you all things, and bring to your remembrance all things that I said to you."
>
> JOHN 14:26 NKJV

What areas are you struggling in today? What do you need help with? The human experience is not easy or linear. There is inevitable pain and suffering that you will experience in this life. You will lose loved ones. You may experience various difficulties. However, there is a great and living hope in Jesus and through his Spirit who dwells with you.

The Spirit is our helper in knowing Jesus. He reveals the deep wisdom of his kingdom and brings to mind the Word of God. He speaks and brings light, life, and freedom. What he does is like no other. He brings refreshment to our souls and strength to our bodies, and he fills us with eternal hope. May you press into the presence of God with you today and find all that you need and more.

Ask the Holy Spirit for fresh revelation of God's kingdom.

Overwhelming Peace

"Peace I leave with you; my peace I give you.
I do not give to you as the world gives.
Do not let your hearts be troubled
and do not be afraid."

JOHN 14:27 NIV

When our hopes are set on the things of this world, the peace and joy that accompany getting them will not last. The desires of this world shift as often as the winds. There is constant change. If we are looking for satisfaction in what we can accomplish or gain in this world, we will be disappointed—if not now, then at some point.

Jesus does not give with conditions attached. He gives freely to all in the same abundant measure. He promises us his peace, the peace of his presence, in all things. When we are afraid, may we turn to him and find our hearts settle in the calming nearness of his lavish love. His peace is stronger than the chaos of any storm. It is purer than water straight from the source of the earth. It is our promised gift. May we extend it to others and live out of its depths.

Promote peace by refusing to gossip.

Clarity

God is not a God of confusion
but of peace.

1 Corinthians 14:33 esv

Have you ever read through Scripture and ended up more confused than when you started? God is not afraid of your questions, and he welcomes you to seek him with all that you are. That includes what puzzles you! The fruit of the Spirit's wisdom is peace, not confusion. Where you have not yet found clarity, God has revelation to break through the fog of your misperceptions.

The truth of God is often simple but profound. Where your mind cannot comprehend the dissonance between what you have known and what you have yet to experience, lean into the presence of God that transcends time. Look to him, even when it is his character that you are questioning. In the light of his mercy, you will find the Living God. He is greater than your limited experience can hold, and he is full of patient love, clarifying wisdom, and true peace. Whatever you do, look to him for the solutions you need. He has an answer for everything.

*When you are confused, ask God for his truth
to break through your understanding.*

My Defense

The LORD is my strength and my defense;
he has become my salvation.
He is my God, and I will praise him,
my father's God, and I will exalt him.

EXODUS 15:2 NIV

Have you ever been so on your guard that you felt as if everything others said was a challenge to prove yourself? In defensiveness, we may misinterpret the concerns of others. We may be unable to hear the heart behind what they present. In fact, what they say may have nothing to do with us at all.

On the other hand, there are times when situations arise that are completely out of our control. Our reputations are slandered, and our integrity may be called into question. In these times, do we fight for ourselves? Do we let others advocate for us? The Lord is our defense, and he will not let rumors run wild, ruining our lives. He will set the record straight, and the truth will be known. Walk in honesty, live rightly and humbly, and trust God with the rest.

*Thank someone who has stood up for you
at some point in your life.*

Simply Remain

"Remain in me, as I also remain in you.
No branch can bear fruit by itself;
it must remain in the vine.
Neither can you bear fruit unless you remain in me."

JOHN 15:4 NIV

The fruit of the Spirit is made manifest in our lives when we live submitted to God. With his love as our leader and his grace as our strength, with his peace as our portion and his joy as our refreshment, we abide in him.

If the fruit we want to bear in our lives is the fruit of God's kingdom, then we must remain in him as he is in us. Do we yield to his voice, following his unmatched wisdom? Do we obey the guidance of his Spirit? When we commit all we do to the Lord, we ask him to take our humble offerings and do with them what only he can do. He is the God who creates rich orchards out of fallow ground. He is the God who brings to life what was desolate on its own. Everything he touches reflects his grandeur and goodness, and our lives are no different.

Commit everything you do today to the Lord.

Lost and Found

> "If a man has a hundred sheep and one of them gets lost, what will he do? Won't he leave the ninety-nine others in the wilderness and go to search for the one that is lost until he finds it?"
>
> Luke 15:4 NLT

No one is dispensable in the kingdom of heaven. Everyone is unique and uniquely loved. Jesus makes this clear in the parable of the lost sheep. God is our Good Shepherd. He is the one who leaves the ninety-nine to find the one wandering sheep. No matter how far from God you feel today, know that his love chases you down. You cannot escape his kindness!

Have you ever lost something that meant a lot to you? Would you not sacrifice your time and energy to find it? You would not leave a pillow unturned or a drawer unchecked. How much more are you worth to God? There is overwhelming joy in reunion. Know that you are loved, you are seen, and you are sought after. The Lord is pursuing you even now.

Reach out to someone you've lost touch with.

Encouraged to Hope

Whatever was written in former days was written for
our instruction, so that by steadfastness and by the
encouragement of the scriptures we might have hope.

ROMANS 15:4 NRSV

Have you ever felt isolated in an experience, convinced
that no one else could understand what you were going
through? Don't let that isolation convince you that you are
alone. There are others who get it, and more than that, God
understands. Jesus lived as a man, though he was God.
He understands both our limitations and our temptations.
In our humanity, though our struggles may look different,
there are general themes that come up time and time again.

May you find courage, hope, and encouragement in
the written Word today. Start in the Psalms, where the
breadth of human experience is expressed through poems
and songs. Whatever it is you are feeling, you will find a
psalm to fit it. There are psalms of victory and psalms of
defeat. There are psalms of lament, psalms of desperation,
and psalms of overwhelming joy. Let your heart find
refreshment in the solidarity you find in the Word.

Read through a few Psalms today.

Sacrificial Love

"The greatest love of all is a love that sacrifices all.
And this great love is demonstrated
when a person sacrifices his life for his friends."

JOHN 15:13 TPT

The greatest love of all isn't a love that requires a lot. It's not a love that stays safe and comfortable inside the walls of its home. It does not hoard, and it is not manipulative. The greatest love of all, as Jesus said, "is a love that sacrifices all."

How have you sacrificed for those you love? How has the love of Jesus moved you to surrender in ways that you may never have chosen on your own? Love moves us outside of our comfort zones into the messiness of the world around us. Love is not tidy. It cannot be wrapped up with a bow. It is always moving, always going further, always reaching. May you be encouraged to stretch yourself in active love today. We only know kindness in the context of relating with others.

Give people preference over your schedule.

Fountain of Hope

May God, the inspiration and fountain of hope, fill you to overflowing with uncontainable joy and perfect peace as you trust in him. And may the power of the Holy Spirit continually surround your life with his super-abundance until you radiate with hope!

ROMANS 15:13 TPT

The Holy Spirit is bursting with abundance in all that we need to radiate with hope. What a beautifully marvelous and transformative relationship we have through God's own Spirit living in us! He has more than enough to fill us to overflowing with joy that cannot be contained and perfect peace that sustains us as we trust in him.

May our lives be continually surrounded by the power of God within us. His merciful kindness is incomparably good. It is wiser than the elitist scholars of this world. He has more to offer us than we could ever need, so let's not hold back from asking and receiving from his generous heart today.

Spend time asking the Holy Spirit to meet you, praying, singing, and meditating on his goodness.

Royal Appointee

"You did not choose Me but I chose you,
and appointed you that you would go and bear fruit,
and that your fruit would remain."

JOHN 15:16 NASB

Before you had any idea of who God was, he knew your name. His own hands formed you; you are the product of his great, creative imagination. He chose you first, and he chooses you still. Will you partner with his heart and yield your life to him? His ways are truer, they are purer, and they are better than any you could imagine creating on your own.

Trust the one who called you and answer his voice today. He is the source of every good thing you have known, and his generous love is the sustenance that will continually transform you into his image. He peels back the layers that keep you stuck and small, and he sets you free in his mercy. You have been appointed and anointed by Christ.

*Thank God for loving you first, for choosing you,
and for being the source of the good gifts in your life.*

Not Too Far

"So he returned home to his father. And while he was still a long way off, his father saw him coming. Filled with love and compassion, he ran to his son, embraced him, and kissed him."

LUKE 15:20 NLT

There is no greater love in this world than the love of God. He is a father. He is a friend. He is our Savior. He is a close confidant. He is pure mercy and kindness at all times. He does not tire of waiting for us to turn and return to him. He always welcomes us as we come to him with open arms. He gives us more than we could ever earn or deserve. He covers our rags with his robe.

What a beautiful God he is! No matter how far we have chosen to roam on our own terms, he always welcomes us back. He does not demean our choices or shame our demise. He is the God of restoration, and he is full of affection for his children. May we not let anything keep us from turning and returning to our good Father. There he is, running toward us whenever we make a move.

Reach out to a loved one you haven't talked to in a while.

Ultimate Victory

"O death, where is your victory?
O death, where is your sting?"

1 CORINTHIANS 15:55 ESV

Perhaps you read the verse for today and feel the defeat of death. Perhaps you feel the sharp sting of loss. Mourning is not ungodly. It is not a more holy route to bypass your pain with positivity that you simply cannot connect to. Let Jesus have access to the messy parts of your heart. He is not afraid of your pain, your questions, or your loss.

Jesus Christ is the victorious one. He defeated death when he rose from the grave on the third day and rose to life. His power has overcome our deepest, darkest fears. He is greater than our understanding. Read the verse again. This time, imagine Jesus saying it. He says it over you, declaring that even in your pain and sorrow, death does not have the final say and never will. Jesus does! His resurrection power is the same power living in you through his Spirit. There is victory, and it does not depend on your happiness. Let Jesus speak his truth over your life.

When you feel defeated, speak God's truth
over your situation.

Through Christ

Thanks be to God!
He gives us the victory
through our Lord Jesus Christ.

1 CORINTHIANS 15:57 NIV

In Christ, all our personal defeats are covered in the overcoming power of his love. He restores what was taken from us, and he redeems the time that we have lost. Where we have done wrong, he leads us in reconciliation and paths of peace. He gives us wisdom about how to humbly restore relationship with those we have hurt.

God never holds against us what he has forgiven. Though we may struggle to forgive ourselves, God fully forgives us when we turn to him and repent. His victory becomes our victory. There is more life ahead than any destruction we leave behind. He is our help, our strength, and our deliverer. He moves in mighty miracles of mercy, and he will not stop! Let's keep our lives surrendered to him, for he is better than any other.

Thank Jesus for his overcoming power today.

Stand Strong

My dear brothers and sisters, stand strong. Do not let anything move you. Always give yourselves fully to the work of the Lord, because you know that your work in the Lord is never wasted.

1 CORINTHIANS 15:58 NCV

"Your work in the Lord is never wasted." Nothing that you do for him goes unnoticed. When you tend to your family, when you fix a meal for a struggling friend, when you take time to listen to another's story at the cost of your own schedule, it is all seen by him. There is no act of love too small or insignificant.

Stand strong in both large ways and small ways. Don't let anything move you from the foundation of Christ's compassion except for Christ himself. Love is not stagnant. It will move you, but that is not the same as turning from your faith. Know that standing strong may sometimes look like moving backward. Follow the leading of love and you will not go astray. Give yourself fully to him and to the work you have to do.

Fix your eyes on Jesus, the author and perfecter of your faith.

He Sees

"The Lord does not see as man sees;
for man looks at the outward appearance,
but the Lord looks at the heart."

1 Samuel 16:7 NKJV

Have you forgotten what matters most to God? It is not how stylish you look; your hair, clothes, and skin do not make an impression on him. He sees your heart, and it is what happens there that matters. What are your motivations? It does not matter how godly your choices may look to others if you are cursing in your heart.

May you realize that your thoughts matter as much to God as anything else. The willingness and humility of your heart also matters. He can see what no one else can; is that good news to you? He can see past all of the struggles to the heart of the matter. When you have experienced his incredible kindness, how could you not extend that to others? Try looking at others the way God does today, and you may find that compassion is discovered in that place.

*Instead of judging someone's appearance,
have a conversation with them.*

Make Him Known

Oh, give thanks to the LORD!
Call upon His name;
Make known His deeds among the peoples!

1 CHRONICLES 16:8 NKJV

Our testimony is where we have seen God move in our lives. How he has met us with his love. How he has transformed what we could never change on our own. How he has moved in wonderfully simple ways and in powerfully elaborate ways. Everyone has a unique story to tell. Some of us have many.

Think back over your walk with God and ask him for perspective to see what you could not in the moment. Ask him to remind you of how he has moved on your behalf. Remember what he has done. There is power in our remembrance, and there is power in the words of our testimonies. Let's use this day to make him known. Let's share with others what he has already done for us. As we do, we may find that our faith grows stronger in the telling and others find their own faith rises in response.

Share a testimony of gratitude with someone today.

Directed by God

A man's heart plans his way,
But the LORD directs his steps.

PROVERBS 16:9 NKJV

It is not a bad thing to make plans and work toward a future you want. This does not mean that you lack faith in God or that you don't trust him to guide you. The fact is, he will guide you as you move. Trust him with your life, don't hold too tightly to the specifics, and walk hand in hand with your Good Shepherd.

Nothing throws him off course. When our own plans are interrupted and we cannot see for the disappointment of our own expectations, he has not stopped guiding us in his goodness. Nothing can upset his confidence. No problem is too large for him. He is bigger than our fears, and he is our faithful leader. Take heart and take hope, no matter where you are on the path of life. The Lord will direct your steps. Trust him!

Thank God for his leadership in your life.

Strength in Courage

Be on your guard;
stand firm in the faith;
be courageous;
be strong.

1 Corinthians 16:13 niv

There is a reason that Scripture warns us to be on our guard. There are temptations along the path of life that would lead us away from resting in the love of God. There are people who may seem like they have our best in mind but are only seeking to manipulate us for their own purposes. The enemy, Peter says, prowls around like a lion looking for someone to devour (1 Peter 5:8).

There is strength found in courage. Our God is with us; his Spirit is our constant companion. May we take courage in God with us, refusing to let fear drive our decisions. May we continually choose to love and to reach out in mercy to others. Let's not become consumed with our own comfort and miss the point of Christ's love altogether. No, let's rise up in the strength of his compassion and trust him to keep us rooted in his faithfulness as we trust in him alone.

Don't let fear drive your decisions today.
Take courage in God!

September

Let us come into his presence
with thanksgiving;
let us make a joyful noise to him
with songs of praise!

PSALM 95:2 NRSV

Spirit of Truth

"When the Spirit of truth comes,
he will guide you into all truth.
He will not speak on his own
but will tell you what he has heard."

JOHN 16:13 NLT

We are not waiting for the Spirit of truth to come to us. He already has! The Spirit of God is the one who guides us into the truth of God's kingdom. Just as Jesus spoke on behalf of the Father, the Spirit speaks on behalf of the Father and Son. They are united and one in love.

If you are struggling to know which way to go, how to make sense of a troubling situation, or what to do in the midst of confusion, ask the Spirit to guide you with his clarifying wisdom. Seek out the advice of trusted advisors. Do what you know to do and be open to letting new information adjust your understanding. Wherever you are, you have access to the fullness of God through his Spirit.

Ask the Spirit to speak to you as you read the Word.

All in Love

Let all that you do be done in love.

1 Corinthians 16:14 NRSV

The overarching theme of love is threaded through the message of Jesus. He spoke of treating others the way we want to be treated. He said that we should love God first and most out of all other things. The way we love others is an overflow of the love we receive from him. Love is not an easy choice when it means turning the other cheek. It is not natural to lay down our defenses.

And yet, that is precisely the kind of love that Jesus calls us to do. It can affect every area of our lives. It is not reserved for the ones we like or for when we are in affable moods. The love of God extends beyond the borders of heaven to transform us. May we choose love in all that we do, humbling ourselves before God and before others.

When you do mundane tasks today,
do them with gratitude in your heart.

Complete Joy

"Until now you have not asked for anything in my name. Ask and you will receive, and your joy will be complete."

JOHN 16:24 NIV

Is there something that you have been hoping for but haven't yet asked for? Jesus was clear that we should ask for more than we do. This is not a magic trick, and it's not a get-out-of-jail-free card. He cares about the things that we care about. He promises that the pain of disappointment we feel is not our inheritance. There is more that he has to offer us in his wisdom than we could imagine, and it is infinitely better than any gift we give each other.

As we get closer to the Lord, may our hearts grow bolder in our prayers. He is always listening, and Jesus himself intercedes for us before the Father. There is joy in his presence, and there is joy in receiving the fullness of his promises. We will taste and see that the Lord is good!

*Thank the Lord for hearing you
and ask him for something specific.*

Loosen Your Grip

"If you try to hang on to your life, you will lose it.
But if you give up your life for my sake, you will save it."

MATTHEW 16:25 NLT

Have you ever been faced with uncomfortable information that you pushed against in denial? Did the act of denying the reality you were faced with help you in the long run? The longer we try to avoid the inevitable, the more we prolong the tension that we feel in trying to control what we cannot. There is relief in the letting go, even though it is painful.

Is there something that you need to release to God today? Is there an area that you've been fighting against, and yet you know that it will not change, no matter how hard you try to manipulate it? There is grace in the presence of God for acceptance. There is mercy to cover your weakness. There is peace in the confidence of his faithfulness, even in the unknowns of tomorrow. He can handle all that you cannot. Dare to trust him with it.

Trust God with the details you cannot control.

Wholly Loved

"The Father himself loves you."

JOHN 16:27 NIV

There is nothing about you that falls outside of the loving embrace of your Father God. He is the one who fights for your freedom, the one who draws you to himself in kindness. Even his correction is lined with love. Though you may struggle to accept the failures you have experienced as valuable, there is nothing that God cannot redeem and restore. He is masterful at using what we deem as wasted to produce beauty in his merciful hands. Even what we see as meaningless is made meaningful in his love.

Will you come to God with the confidence of a dearly loved child today? He welcomes you with open arms, and he longs to speak his words of life over you. Take some time to listen to what he is saying. He will silence the lies with his truth. He will calm the chaos of uncertainty with his peace. He will love you to life again if you let him.

Thank the Father for his love.

Overcomers

"I have said these things to you, that in me you may
have peace. In the world you will have tribulation.
But take heart; I have overcome the world."

JOHN 16:33 ESV

Jesus knows us so well. He knows the weakness of our
mortality and the short memories we have. He realizes that
when troubles come, we will go into our natural responses:
fight, flight, or freeze. He does not belittle or demean us in
our humanity. Rather, he gives us warning and reminds us
time and time again to look to him for our confidence and
peace.

Though we walk through various difficulties in this life,
Jesus has already overcome them all. Their power to
produce fear is not greater than the power of God's
perfect peace. When we are in seasons of struggle, let's
remember Jesus' words and take heart in his promises.
He has overcome the world, and we can find true peace
in his presence even in the midst of our suffering. What a
wonderful Savior he is! What a wonderful God! Let's look
to Jesus more than any other. He is faithful, he is true, and
he is the hope of our salvation.

In the face of troubles, take heart!
Jesus has already overcome them.

He Is Good

Give thanks to the LORD, for he is good
his love endures forever.

1 CHRONICLES 16:34 NIV

Are you familiar with this benediction? "God is good all
the time. All the time, God is good." Some of us may
have grown up repeating this so often that it has lost
its meaning. Others of us may have struggled to realize
that God is good at all. Whatever our views of God in our
traditions, may we be challenged to look for the evidence
of God's goodness in our lives.

His love endures forever. Where there is evidence of love
in our lives, there is the fruit of God's goodness. Take some
time to look for the fingerprints of mercy in your story.
Where has God met you with his grace? What things were
you worried about that later resolved? When have you felt
overwhelmed by gratitude? Give thanks to the Lord. He is
good, and his love endures forever!

Where you see goodness in your life, give thanks to God.

Childlike Faith

Jesus called for the children, saying,
"Let the little children come to me.
Don't stop them, because the kingdom of God
belongs to people who are like these children."

LUKE 18:16 NCV

Children are natural questioners. They are full of curiosity, and they say whatever is on their minds. We are not meant to come to God with perfect manners and compliance. He welcomes us with all our energy, our passion, and our inquisitiveness. He does not shut down our active imaginations or discourage our questions. Praise God for that!

Approach Jesus freely with unhindered curiosity. He welcomes you as you are, and he delights in your unbridled joy. Where you have grown cynical, lay down the armor of self-protection and let him in. Ask him the hardest questions you have. Hold nothing back! He is able and willing to entertain each one. Oh, how he loves you, and how he longs to fellowship with you.

Let go of cynicism and ask God for his perspective.

There He Is

"If two or three people come together in my name,
I am there with them."

MATTHEW 18:20 NIV

We are not meant to live isolated from others. We were made to thrive in relationships. Think of the last time you had a really good conversation with a loved one. Did it not encourage your soul? Was it not refreshing to your heart? Do you see the importance of relating to others in authenticity and love? It is an invitation to deeper awareness, greater compassion, and shared joy.

God is not excluded from our relationships. When we gather in his name, no matter where we are or what we are doing, he is there in the fellowship. There is encouragement, there is power, and there is life in community. May we not forget the importance of fellowship for our whole health. Our souls, spirits, and bodies are refreshed and revived in the company of loving friendship.

Meet with a friend to pray and catch up.

Sought After

"The Son of Man has come to seek and to save
that which was lost."

LUKE 19:10 NKJV

No matter how far we feel we have strayed, God is undeterred in his love toward us. He is the Shepherd who leaves the masses of the safe to seek out the one lost, vulnerable lamb. He does not give up on those he loves, so do not disqualify yourself or anyone else based on your ideas of worthiness. After all, he turns coal to diamonds.

Jesus Christ is the same yesterday, today, and forever. He is not going to cast away the worn out or the defenseless. He goes to the edges of society and speaks his life over them. He is not too holy to show up in the most unexpected of places. Wherever you are, know that God pursues you with his fiery love. Turn to him, for he is near.

Recognize that no matter where you are today,
you are not out of God's reach.

Endless Possibilities

Jesus looked at them and said to them,
"With men this is impossible,
but with God all things are possible."

MATTHEW 19:26 NKJV

Nothing is impossible for God. No matter how many limitations you experience, God has none. He is able to do far more than you could ever imagine asking him to do. He is able to save, redeem, and restore. With God, all things are possible.

Are there any areas of your life that feel unbearable? Are there any struggles that you just can't seem to shake? Look to the God who calms raging seas. The same God will calm the intense fear inside of you with his perfect peace. Pray to him, laying your heart bare before him. Dare to trust that what he says, he will do. He is faithful and true, and he will not fail to meet you with his tangible mercy. Don't despair, for his resources are endless.

Thank God for his ability to do the impossible.

Run to Him

My God is my rock.
I can run to him for safety.
The Lord saves me from those who want to harm me.

2 Samuel 22:3 ncv

God is our security, our refuge, and a safe place to run in our times of trouble. His presence wraps around us like a warm blanket, comforting us and keeping us close in his love. He welcomes the weak and the vulnerable. He is a safe space for the refugee. He is the peace that every traumatized heart is looking for.

Do we look like the image of love in the way that we interact with the displaced, the immigrant, and the poor? Do we embrace all with the same love that God does? Or do we reject some in favor of those who make us feel comfortable? As we run to God time and time again, may we become people who reflect him as we welcome the weak and protect the vulnerable.

Ask God how you can be a safe place for the vulnerable.

Rest on Every Side

"Is not the LORD your God with you? And has He not given you rest on every side? For He has given the inhabitants of the land into my hand, and the land is subdued before the LORD and before His people."

1 CHRONICLES 22:19 NKJV

The Lord our God is with us where we are, and where the Spirit of the Lord is, there is also his perfect peace. He gives us rest. In rest we find renewal, and in renewal we are able to keep moving in his love.

No one is meant to run on empty or hustle their way into the kingdom. That's not how it works. He offers us rest when the world demands more than we can give. The expectations of others never cease, but we don't live to please others. We live to please God! It pleases God when we rest in his presence, and we are more able to walk his path of love when we have been filled with the refreshing peace we find in rest.

Spend twenty minutes resting without looking at your phone.

Upside-down Kingdom

"Who is the greater, one who reclines at table or one who serves? Is it not the one who reclines at table? But I am among you as the one who serves."

LUKE 22:27 ESV

In a world where the greater your name is, the more pampered you are, it is refreshing to know that Jesus, the King of all creation, came to serve. He is the pinnacle of servant leadership, laying down his life so that we could know the extent of the Father's love. He is the living example of God's love, and he is our example.

May we never forget the importance of reaching out to others in love. As we look for opportunities to serve each other in both little and large ways, we become reflections of Jesus' glorious light. Where pride inflates our sense of importance, humility keeps us close to Jesus. Let's be like him in how we assist one another.

Look for ways to serve someone today.

Perfect Ways

This God—his way is perfect;
the word of the LORD proves true;
he is a shield for all those who take refuge in him.

2 SAMUEL 22:31 ESV

The ways of the Lord are far above our best days. He is perfect in all of his ways, and his character is completely unchanging. He is full of compassion, kindness, and mercy. He is full of strength, power, and justice. He is true, he is eternal, and he is the same from age to age.

When we feel as if we are losing our way, we can ground ourselves in the unshakable nature of Jesus. He is the perfect representation of the Father to us. He is our shield and refuge. Let's run into his gracious presence and receive everything that we need. He is our peace, he is our confidence, and he is our advocate. All his ways are perfect, and we can trust him at all times.

Imitate God's character in your choices today.

Vows of Faithfulness

"God is not man, that he should lie, or a son of man, that he should change his mind. Has he said, and will he not do it? Or has he spoken, and will he not fulfill it?"

NUMBERS 23:19 ESV

The faithfulness of God cannot be overstated. He does not manipulate us or deceive us. He does not flatter us or spin a web of lies. He is true in all things. He is the source of goodness. He is divine love.

When we are tempted to doubt God's goodness, let's go to him. He is not afraid of our questions, and he does not turn us away when we waver. Instead of letting doubt pull us from his presence, let's press in further with all of our baggage. After all, he is the lifter of our burdens. What a wonderful God he is! Let's bring him everything we have and refresh ourselves in communion with his Spirit. His promises are sure.

Speak God's promises over your doubt.

Opened Understanding

Then he opened their minds
to understand the Scriptures.

LUKE 24:45 ESV

Without the help of God, can we really understand the
vast goodness of his wisdom? We love because he first
loved us. We believe him because he births faith within us.
We are connected to him because he reached out to us to
draw us to himself.

Is there a question that you have been wrestling with? Is
there a problem you have not been able to solve? Ask the
Lord to illuminate your understanding. Ask the Spirit to
open your mind to his revelation. Every time he does, deep
knowing of his truth responds from within. What once was
clouded becomes clear. There is nothing that we cannot
ask God to help us with. May we press in even further,
asking him to speak directly to us through his Word.

Before you read the Scriptures today,
ask God to open your mind to his wisdom.

Wonderful Things

Lord, you are my God;
I will exalt you and praise your name,
for in perfect faithfulness
you have done wonderful things,
things planned long ago.

Isaiah 25:1 niv

What wonderful things have you experienced in your walk with the Lord? What has he done that no one else could do for you? How has he helped you through a difficult time? Look at your story through the lens of curiosity. Ask God to reveal where he was working in it with his mercy that brings life out of the ashes of defeat.

After our lives have settled, we often forget the prayers we prayed in our desperation. We tend to remember the negative. What if we look for where prayers were answered, peace was bestowed, and all was well in the end? Perhaps we will find a broader picture of God's mercy in our lives than we remembered. He is good, and he leads us into life. Ask the Spirit to remind you of worries long forgotten because of God's faithfulness. Maybe there, you'll find courage and hope for your present troubles.

Praise God for his fulfilled promises in your life.

Reliable Defense

You have been a defense for the helpless,
A defense for the needy in his distress,
A refuge from the storm, a shade from the heat;
For the breath of the ruthless is like a rain storm
against a wall.

ISAIAH 25:4 NASB

How has God been a shelter for you in times of trouble?
Have you seen his hand of protection over your life in
specific instances? Even if you cannot pinpoint one in this
moment, let your mind meditate on his sovereignty. God is
unflappable. He is unshakable. He is full of loyal love, and he
guards his children like a good shepherd guards his flock.

Whatever trouble you are facing, you can take it to the
Lord. Whatever distress you are feeling, he can handle
every bit of it. He is not overwhelmed by your messy
emotions. He welcomes you as you are, and he covers you
in the cloak of his loving kindness. Press into the safety of
his side, for he is your protector and your place of rest. Run
into him whenever you feel unsure.

Write down how God has defended you and kept you safe.

Peace of Mind

You keep him in perfect peace
whose mind is stayed on you,
because he trusts in you.

ISAIAH 26:3 ESV

Have worries got you overwhelmed? Do you fight the urge to figure out how to control the situations that feel insurmountable? There is too much to face in this world where new tragedies are reported every day. However, there is a port of peace in the presence of God with us. His peace is not fickle, nor is it fragile.

Turn your thoughts to Jesus whenever you feel the talons of anxiety clawing at you. Look to him, meditate on his Word, and remember his faithfulness. He is nearer than you know, so take heart! He always leads in loving clarity and settles our hearts with his perfect peace. When you don't know what else to do, let the prayers of your heart connect you to the Spirit of God that is already close. He will keep you in perfect peace when you turn your attention toward him. Put your trust in him, for he will not fail you.

Keep bringing your thoughts back to God's faithfulness
throughout your day.

The Everlasting Way

Search me, God, and know my heart;
test me and know my anxious thoughts.
See if there is any offensive way in me,
and lead me in the way everlasting.

PSALM 139:23-24 NIV

The Lord knows us completely. When we invite his wisdom and leadership, we open ourselves up to his lifegiving words. He course-corrects those who look to him. No matter how lost we may feel, God is never at a loss. He always sees a way out, provides clarity for our confusion, and redirects us as we take hold of his hand.

Are we living for our own purposes, overwhelmed by the pull for more and lacking satisfaction? Today is the perfect opportunity to invite God to search our hearts. As he tests us and sees our anxious thoughts, he can speak life and correction to us. When we look at our problems in the light of his presence, what was cloudy becomes clear. We can trust God to lead us into his life again and again. His way is everlasting.

Invite the Lord to search your heart
and redirect you in his love.

Do the Work

"Be strong and courageous, and do the work.
Don't be afraid or discouraged, for the LORD God,
my God, is with you. He will not fail you or forsake you.
He will see to it that all the work related to the Temple
of the LORD is finished."

1 CHRONICLES 28:20 NLT

Whatever work you have to do, do it unto the Lord. He has not called you to live a life that is disconnected from responsibilities or reality. In your tasks, God is present. When he leads you, he provides all the strength you need. When you follow the path laid out for you, he will never leave you to get through on your own. There is work for you to do, and the presence of the Lord is with you in it.

Everything that you do for the Lord matters. Every act of courage and strength you perform, moving forward in the work he has given you to do, is worthwhile. He sees it all Trust him to be with you through it all. He won't ever abandon you, and he will take care of the details you cannot.

*Put energy into your work with a thankful heart,
knowing God is with you in it.*

Constant Companionship

"I am with you always,
even to the end of the age."

Matthew 28:20 nasb

Jesus' promise to his followers that he would be with them "even to the end of the age" also applies to us today. After he ascended to the Father, he sent the Spirit, who is the fullness of God without form. When we surrender our lives to Christ, we are given full access to the Father through fellowship with the Spirit with us.

No matter what you are going through, you are not alone. No matter how isolated you feel, you are not alone. No matter the depth of your struggles, you are not alone. God himself is with you in the Spirit. The Holy Spirit is your constant companion through every high and every low, through storms and in seasons of celebration. Slow down in the present moment, inviting the peace of his presence to fill your heart, mind, soul, and body. He is ever so near!

Thank God for his presence that never leaves.

Only a Moment

We are here for only a moment, visitors and strangers in the land as our ancestors were before us. Our days on earth are like a passing shadow, gone so soon without a trace.

1 CHRONICLES 29:15 NLT

This life is fleeting. Though we may live through seasons where we feel invincible, the truth of the matter is that we are only passing through like travelers in a strange land. May we embrace the time we have and use every opportunity to choose to live with love, kindness, and purpose.

What is the underlying motivation through your days, weeks, months, and years? What vision are you moving toward? What values drive you? Take the time to sift out unhelpful habits that don't serve you or others well and keep those you want to prioritize in your one life. How do you want to be known by those closest to you? What do you want your legacy to be? Take the opportunity you have, here and now, to choose how you will live. It is yours to do!

Choose kindness even when you are frustrated.

All Is His

"O Lᴏʀᴅ our God, all this abundance that we have
provided to build You a house for Your holy name,
it is from Your hand, and all is Yours."

1 Cʜʀᴏɴɪᴄʟᴇs 29:16 ɴᴀsʙ

May we give to God with hearts that are full of gratitude.
May we have a revelation of the goodness of God,
recognizing that what we have is what he has given to
us. There is nothing in this world that remains outside the
realm of his merciful kindness. Let us reflect the beauty
and bounty of God's generosity toward us by offering him
our resources.

There is power in the practice of open-handed generosity.
When we sense a desire to hoard what we have for
ourselves, may we turn to the Lord and give him access
to our hearts. Let's ask him for a fresh revelation of the
largeness of his kingdom. As we stay humble in his love,
our offerings will flow from a place of devotion and trust.

*Give back to God a portion of what you have,
thanking him for his generosity.*

Dawning Compassion

The LORD longs to be gracious to you;
therefore he will rise up to show you compassion.
For the LORD is a God of justice.
Blessed are all who wait for him!

ISAIAH 30:18 NIV

"The Lord longs to be gracious to you." Meditate on that for a moment. The gracious heart of God longs to be meet you right where you are. Soak in the truth of his loving kindness that reaches toward you. The grace of God motivates his every movement. "Therefore he will rise up to show you compassion." He will not neglect to come to you as you wait on him. His love never fails.

Whatever stress you have been under, whatever weight you have been feeling, know that the compassion of the Lord dawns upon his children! He does not ignore the cries of his beloved ones, and he will not ignore their difficulties. Wait upon him, for he is at work in the details of your story. He will not let you down!

Wait on God until you feel his peace and love.

Walk Here

Your ears shall hear a word behind you, saying,
"This is the way, walk in it,"
Whenever you turn to the right hand
or whenever you turn to the left."

ISAIAH 30:21 NKJV

God is more involved in our lives than we can know. When we ask him to direct our choices, he will lead us in his wisdom. When we come to the proverbial fork in the road, he will guide us when we listen for his voice. We need not rely solely on our own logic; we can also lean on the wonderful leadership of the Spirit with us.

What would it look like to practice hearing the voice of the Lord in your decision-making? The Spirit knows us so well. When we ask for the Lord's input on our choices, we can trust his heart for us. We always have freedom to select what we will, for that is what free will is all about. We also have the opportunity to listen to the leadership of the Lord at all times. May we learn to trust him even as we take responsibility for our choices.

Ask God to direct your choices today.

No Wrong

He is the Rock, his works are perfect,
and all his ways are just.
A faithful God who does no wrong,
upright and just is he.

DEUTERONOMY 32:4 NIV

Though we cannot find anyone in this world who perfectly embodies the kingdom of God, we have the Lord as our solid foundation. Everything he does is just, merciful, and right. Jesus is the way, the truth, and the life. He is faithful in loving kindness, and he is powerful in resurrection strength. There is nothing that he cannot do!

When we are tempted to stoop to the level of those who would rather throw blame than take responsibility for their actions, let's look to the example of Jesus. As we follow him on the pathway of his love, there is no excuse for bitterness. May we allow the purity of his compassion to change us from the inside out. He is our help in all things, including in extending mercy to those we struggle to offer it to in our own strength.

Instead of excusing your lack of love,
ask God to help you choose his ways.

Never Lost

He found them in a desert,
a windy, empty land.
He surrounded them and brought them up,
guarding them as those he loved very much.

DEUTERONOMY 32:10 NCV

No matter where we find ourselves in this life, we are never out of sight from God. He sees us, and he knows exactly where we are even if we are unable to discern it for ourselves. He surrounds us with his kindness, and he guards us with his mercy. When we are in the desert, with barrenness as our only vision, may we sense the nearness of our Good Shepherd.

Have you felt lost lately? Perhaps you are out of the wilderness, but you vividly remember what it felt like. Look to God today and remember his faithfulness. He has not left you yet, and he never will. May his Spirit remind you of the deposits of his kindness that have kept you along your journey so far. He is still leading you in his compassion even now.

Write a poem of thanks to God for his protection.

Safe and Secure

"My people will live free from worry in secure,
quiet homes of peace."

ISAIAH 32:18 TPT

Have you found your peaceful home in Christ? Have you experienced the rest of his presence, where worries are laid down and trust is built up? In the fellowship of the Spirit, we experience the overwhelming peace of his nearness. His comfort moves and quiets our souls.

Whatever troubles you have been facing, may you know that you are safe and secure in the love of God. He is your refuge and your sustenance. He is full of refreshing springs to revive your weary heart. He does not leave you to be overwhelmed by your circumstances. He is with you in every trial and in every storm. He is as confident and sure in your darkest night as he is on your brightest day. May you find deep rest for your soul in his presence. Lay down your heavy burdens and take his hand. He will gently tuck you into the crook of his arm where you are safe and secure.

Write down areas of your life in which you feel secure and safe.

October

I will praise you, Lord, with all my heart;
I will tell of all the marvelous things
you have done.

PSALM 9:1 NLT

Unchanging Purposes

The plans of the Lord stand firm forever,
the purposes of his heart through all generations.

PSALM 33:11 NIV

The purposes of God's heart never change. They are consistent, and he is constantly working on them in our lives and in the world. He is full of mercy and loving kindness that meets us where we are. He moves rightly, and he will not neglect his justice. What he set out to do in the beginning, he is still doing in every generation.

Oh, that we would recognize the continual thread of his mercy throughout the generations! That we would have eyes to see and ears to hear how his goodness has brought people through dark nights and deep valleys into the wide-open fields of his gracious favor. God is unchanging in the motivations of his love. He does not shift with the winds or currents of this world. He is immovable in righteousness. He is a sure and unshakable foundation for us to build our lives upon.

Take an opportunity to follow through on your word today.

Everlasting Support

The eternal God is your refuge,
and underneath are the everlasting arms.

DEUTERONOMY 33:27 NIV

When our legs give way under the weight of our worries,
God is there to hold us up. He never leaves us in our
despair, and he becomes our wrap-around shield and safe
place. When we are weak, the strength of the Lord rises up
to meet us. His arms hold us close, and they do not give
way underneath us. He will not drop us.

God is eternal, forever full of power that overcomes our
fears. He does not grow weak, and he does not tire of
us. His patience is greater than we can imagine. His hope
never dwindles, so let us bring our fading hopes to him
to be fueled by his fresh fire. May we find ourselves loved
to life in the comfort of his presence when our weariness
is overwhelming. He leads us to rivers of refreshment in
his Spirit. He gives living waters of his love to revive our
drained hearts.

Give God your worries.

Always Praise

I will praise the LORD at all times;
his praise is always on my lips.

PSALM 34:1 NCV

In all things, at all times, there is always a reason to offer
praise to the Living God. Praise him, for his mercies never
end! Praise him, for he meets us with the power of his love
in overwhelming measure when we look to him. Praise him,
for he is with you even in your deepest pain and suffering.

May praises rise from your heart in an unending stream
of thanksgiving. Cultivate a heart of gratitude, and it will
flow more easily. Thank him for his constant presence.
Thank him for his clarifying wisdom. Let it be personal. No
detail is too small. No answered prayer is too miniscule.
No offering of praise is insignificant. It all counts, and he
recognizes each one. Praise him, for he is yours and you
are his. Let all that is within you offer grateful praise to
your God and King.

*Praise God throughout your day, giving him thanks
for who he is and what he has done.*

Abounding in Mercy

"The Lord, the Lord,
a God merciful and gracious,
slow to anger,
and abounding in steadfast love and faithfulness."

Exodus 34:6 nrsv

In the constant and steadfast love of God, he is slow to anger. He sees the motivations of every heart, the hurt and defensiveness we act upon in our reactions to others. He knows the limits of our humanity, and he extends mercy toward us in unending measure. There is nothing we do that he does not understand. Even when we do not see the root of our anger, he sees it clearly.

If we are to be like Christ, one of the ways we can practice becoming more like him is to take everything to the Father in prayer. There is nothing that we cannot say to God. He knows our hearts already. Let's come to the Father of generous grace, and let's pour out our hearts to him. Let's give him our rage and our confusion. He brings clarity with his presence.

Ask God to give you insight into your anger;
lay down the need to be right.

On the Way

Say to those with fearful hearts,
"Be strong, and do not fear,
for your God...is coming to save you."

ISAIAH 35:4 NLT

When fear fills us, we can respond in multiple ways. We may fight it, flee from it, or freeze when confronted by it. No matter our response, there is a force greater than fear; it is the perfect love of God. His presence permeates our souls, giving us courage in the face of overwhelming odds.

God is our help, our mighty defender, and our strength when we are weak. No matter how beaten down and frail we feel when anxiety fills our bodies, God's perfect peace comes in the calming force of his presence. He settles our systems with the truth of his love. He is with us. He never leaves us. He is our Savior, our Redeemer, and our restorer. Let us look to him and take courage. Help is on the way!

Write down your fears.
Ask God to speak his truth over them.

Good Shepherd

He takes care of his people like a shepherd.
He gathers them like lambs in his arms
and carries them close to him.
He gently leads the mothers of the lambs.

ISAIAH 40:11 NCV

The Lord's leadership is like a gentle shepherd who guides us into green pastures. He does not force us to keep in line with stringent standards. He is not a dictator who demands loyal servitude without question. He is the Good Shepherd who gathers the little lambs close. His sheep learn the tone and timbre of his voice. Though we may stray, he finds us and leads us back to the protection of his watchful care and the grasses that are good for us.

Have you known God as your Shepherd? He longs to lead you along the paths of his quiet waters. He wants to restore your soul in the calm brooks of his bliss. Will you follow him today? Listen for his voice and move toward it when you hear him.

Thank God for his gentle leadership in your life.

Called by Name

Lift up your eyes on high
And see who has created these stars,
The One who leads forth their host by number,
He calls them all by name;
Because of the greatness of His might
and the strength of His power,
Not one of them is missing.

ISAIAH 40:26 NASB

The same God who placed each star in the heavens is the God who created you. He put you together with purpose. He knows the number of hairs on your head, and he knows the hidden talents that others don't see. He knows the values that feed your life, and he put that drive within you. You are unique, and you are uniquely his. There is no one else like you in the entire world, and there never will be again.

May you find strength, belonging, and purpose in the heart of God. He loves you because he created you! He did not make a mistake when he formed your face, and he didn't slip up when he put your personality together. You are intimately known by your Creator, and you are a delight to his heart!

Go outside tonight and look at the stars,
remembering their Creator is yours too.

He Doesn't Tire

"Do you not know? Have you not heard? The Lᴏʀᴅ is the everlasting God, the Creator of the ends of the earth. He will not grow tired or weary, and his understanding no one can fathom."

ISAIAH 40:28 NIV

In our mortal bodies, it is difficult to imagine never growing tired. In the twenty-four hours of a day, we work, eat, and sleep, and we begin again the next day. Without enough water, food, or rest, we do not function well. We were created for rhythms of restoration, and that includes feeding our bodies, minds, and souls. God, however, is the fullness of life. He never grows tired or irritable.

May you find encouragement in the strength of the Lord, not shame in your weakness. The Lord is your Creator, and he is well aware of your limits. He didn't create you to burn out by never resting. No one can fathom his wisdom. Are you lacking insight? Ask him; he has perfect perception. Lean on his strength and rest in his perfection.

In your weariness, realize that God is greater and never tires of helping you.

More Power

He gives strength to those who are tired
and more power to those who are weak.

ISAIAH 40:29 NCV

When we have nothing left to offer in our own strength, the grace of God empowers us to keep going. This is not to say we should not prioritize rest when we can. But sometimes, that is not enough. In some seasons, we do not have the opportunities for deep rest and refreshment as in others. In those times, let us lean into the power of God with us.

The Spirit is our help in all things. He gives us the tenacity we need to hold on when we would rather give up. He helps us to press on when we would rather stop. No matter what, he holds us. He rises up on our behalf. His strength is made perfect in our weakness, meaning he is able to do far more in our submission than in our resistance. Let's hold on to him as he holds on to us.

Ask God for more strength and power where you have nothing left to give.

Wait on His Strength

Those who wait for the LORD shall renew their strength,
they shall mount up with wings like eagles,
they shall run and not be weary,
they shall walk and not faint.

ISAIAH 40:31 NRSV

Anxiety can keep us moving at a frenetic pace rather than taking time to reset and wait on the wisdom of God. When fear rushes us ahead, let's be mindful of the pace at which we're going. Instead of being hasty in our nervousness, let's take the time to slow down and become present in the current moment.

The love of God does not poke or prod us. It does not rush us. The pace of God is steady and sure. When we wait upon the Lord, we will find our strength renewed in his presence. When it is time to move ahead, we will rise up with the power of his Spirit's strength within us, refreshed and revived. In his timing, we find that we have everything we need along the way with no need to worry about where his provision will come from. We learn to rest in him, and he becomes our confidence.

Take some time to rest and wait on God today.

Held Up

Don't be afraid, for I am with you.
Don't be discouraged, for I am your God.
I will strengthen you and help you.
I will hold you up with my victorious right hand.

ISAIAH 41:10 NLT

In your discouragement, do not give way to despair. In your disappointment, do not forget who God is. He is loyal in love, and he restores all things. He is help to the needy, and he gives strength to the weak. He upholds those whose knees buckle under the weight of worry. Let's give him our heavy burdens. He can handle them, and he knows just what to do with them.

When you are afraid, remember that God is with you. When you are weak, know that the power to revive you is through his Spirit who lives within you. You do not need to rely on your own abilities, reflexes, and strengths to bring you victory over fear. God's love will do that for you. Lean on his presence and fill up on his fresh mercies that are new every time you turn to him.

Remember a time when God helped you
and thank him for it.

Unstoppable

"I know that you can do anything,
and no one can stop you."

JOB 42:2 NLT

The Lord's power is greater than any other force in the universe. His love motivates his every move, and when he establishes his justice, no one can overturn it. Nothing is impossible for him. Is there something so completely out of your control that you can't even find the words to pray? Ask God to do the impossible for you.

There's no need to lay out a plan on behalf of God. You need not dictate how he will move. Ask him to do what he does best, and then rest in trust. No one can stop the Lord's mercy once it is in motion. Nothing can stand in the way of his resurrection power. May you know the peace of his presence. The incredible power of his life is in yours. Ask him for help, believe that he will, and trust him to do it. He is unstoppable!

Pray for the impossible situations in your life.

Redeemed by Love

"I have redeemed you;
I have called you by name;
you are Mine!"

ISAIAH 43:1 NASB

Where we find our identity will affect how we live. When we know who we belong to and where we come from, we can own the power of our heritage. It doesn't matter what our earthly family looks like or the beauty or mess that we come from. When we come to Jesus, he welcomes us into his family.

When we yield our lives to Christ, our Redeemer, we find our identity in who he says that we are. He is the one who speaks over us: "I have redeemed you; I have called you by name; you are Mine!" We belong to the King of kings and Lord of lords! We belong to Most High, Creator of the universe. We belong to him! He has called us each by name. We are called out, chosen, restored in his perfect love, wrapped up in his mercy, and released into our destinies to live as his children. Hallelujah!

Live as a child of love, reflecting God's kindness.

Irreversible Mercy

"Even from eternity I am He,
and there is none who can deliver out of My hand;
I act and who can reverse it?"

ISAIAH 43:13 NASB

What God does, no one can reverse. In his power, he moves in mercy toward all that he has made. He is the God who saves the vulnerable and who sets the lonely in families. He is the God of the down and out, the God who reaches to the edges of society, the God who welcomes the poor as openly as anyone else.

Let's dig into the marvelous mercy of our God revealed through Scripture today. Let's look at the life, ministry, and words of Jesus that reveal the heart of the Father to us. Even from eternity, Christ is the Living God. He acts, and no one can reverse it. What are the acts of Jesus? What did he do? What was the main message of his ministry? What effect does that have on our lives and how we should live?

*Read through Jesus' Sermon on the Mount
to understand his mercy better.*

In the Wilderness

"I am about to do something new.
See, I have already begun! Do you not see it?
I will make a pathway through the wilderness.
I will create rivers in the dry wasteland."

ISAIAH 43:19 NLT

Even when life leads us through a wilderness season where everything is dry and dusty, God is with us. He makes pathways through the wilderness. He leads us with the confidence of his constant presence and his consistent kindness.

When God does something new, it requires us to trust him. He leads us into unknown territory where we do not know the lay of the land. He always knows which way to go. Let us depend on his perspective more than our own lack of understanding. We will not die of thirst, for he creates rivers in the desert. He knows where each source of our strength and hope is going to come from. Let's fix our eyes on Jesus and follow him into the new territory of our faith.

*Give God your fears and fix your attention
on his goodness today.*

Come Home

"I have swept away offences like a cloud,
your sins like the morning mist.
Return to me, for I have redeemed you."

ISAIAH 44:22 NIV

Is there anything that has been keeping you from turning to the Lord? Has there been something that has held you back from receiving the fullness of his forgiveness? Come to him today; return to him. He is like the father of the prodigal son who, seeing his son from a far way off, ran to meet him. He welcomes you with open arms, and he wraps his robes of mercy around you.

When you are ready to come to him, he is ready with an embrace. He will not scold or shame you. He will not tell you, "I told you so." He is gentle and kind even in his correction. You will know the restoration power of his love as you return to him. Throw off the fear of rejection, for he is for you and your restoration. Come home. Your father waits for you.

Come to God without hesitation. He welcomes you!

Hidden Treasures

"I will give you hidden treasures,
riches stored in secret places,
so that you may know that I am the Lord,
the God of Israel, who summons you by name."

ISAIAH 45:3 NIV

Even in the darkest nights of the soul, the Lord gives us access to hidden treasures. There are riches that we will only discover in the secret cover of darkness. Let's not despair when grief tears at our souls. In the ripping open, there is also an expansion of our capacity to know God's love in greater measure. His love is uncontainable, and yet it is like flowing water that fills the capacity of our cups.

In the dark caverns under the earth, pressure turns coal to diamonds. In the pressures of life, in the dark caverns of sorrow and grief, we are transformed in the glory of God's presence with us. It is from the discomfort of sand in an oyster that a pearl is produced. Don't despise the discomfort of your circumstance, for it will turn to beauty in the end.

Ask God to show you where treasures have formed in the darkness of your pain.

Relief in Him

Sing for joy. For the LORD has comforted his people and will have compassion on them in their suffering.

ISAIAH 49:13 NLT

When we are burdened by the hardness of life, God is our comfort. When unexpected tragedies lead us into deep grief, God is with us in the pain and suffering. Jesus knows what it is like to suffer. He was a man of many sorrows, handed over to those who wanted his life for a few silver coins. He knows what suffering is. He lived it himself.

The Spirit of God is our very present help in times of trouble. He is our very near comfort in times of mourning. He is with us. He gives us relief in his presence. He mourns with us, holds us close, and speaks tenderly to our hearts. There is no need to rush into feeling better. Let us hold onto him and take the time and space we need to grieve our losses. He is ever so near, our Emmanuel—God with us.

Thank God for his nearness in suffering.

Not Ashamed

The Lord God helps me,
Therefore, I am not disgraced;
Therefore, I have set my face like flint,
And I know that I will not be ashamed.

ISAIAH 50:7 NASB

When the Lord calls us forth in faith, may we set our faces like flint and walk in the confidence of his faithfulness. We will not be disgraced when we depend on him. We will not be put to shame when we follow the pathway of his love. Even if things seem to fall apart on the outside, we know that the one who called us is faithful and true, and he will not abandon us.

The Lord God helps us. He is the one who feeds us with his presence, giving us strength to persevere through the trials of this life. He is our constant companion through everything, both the hills and the valleys. He is with us in the brightness of the noon sun, and he is with us in the darkness of a moonless night. May we stake our confidence on the character of God and rely on him through everything.

Trust what God has said and walk confidently in his steps.

Heart of Surrender

My sacrifice, O God, is a broken spirit;
a broken and contrite heart you, God, will not despise.

PSALM 51:17 NIV

Instead of offering the overflow of our excess to God, let's give him the first fruits of our hearts and lives. When we surrender to him, submitting to his leadership in our lives, we allow his love to guide us. This sounds easy, but it is not. It isn't easy, but it is simple. Let's keep our hearts connected to him through humble submission.

We don't need to belittle ourselves or beat ourselves up for making mistakes. God is not looking for perfect followers. He just wants our willingness to know him and to be known by him. He wants a living relationship. There is give and take in relationships. What will we offer him? Will we offer what he does not want or even ask for? Or will we give him what he requires—a heart that is open to him and willing to be led in his ways.

Offer Jesus access to your heart today.

Finished

Because it is finished
I will be praising you forever and giving you thanks.
Before all your godly lovers I will proclaim your
beautiful name!

PSALM 52:9 TPT

Christ has done everything necessary to clear the way to the Father. The finished work of the cross is all that we need to look to. He is the door, and all who enter through relationship with him find themselves in the fullness of God's mercy. There is nothing to add to what he has already accomplished, and there is nothing that can take away from the power of his resurrection life.

Today, lay aside everything that has kept you from coming to Jesus. Can you give him your full attention for a few minutes? You don't need to get your emotions under control or feel full of faith to approach him. He is full of loyal love toward you right now, and he welcomes you with the generosity of his gracious heart.

Give God a few minutes of undistracted time today.

Unfailing Love

"Though the mountains be shaken and the hills be removed, yet my unfailing love for you will not be shaken nor my covenant of peace be removed," says the LORD, who has compassion on you.

ISAIAH 54:10 NIV

Even when everything that can be shaken in this world is quaking, the love of the Lord remains unshakable. He is as steadfast in mercy in this moment as he ever has been or ever will be. He will always keep his promises.

When God makes a covenant, he never goes back on it. The covenant of his peace with us through Christ is a forever promise. It is a vow that he will keep. His compassion is evident through the life, ministry, and the sacrifice of Christ. His power is made clear through the resurrection of his body from the grave. There is nothing that can keep his unfailing love from meeting us where we are. Don't despair, for the fullness of Christ's mercy and kindness is yours today and forever.

Thank God for his reliable and faithful love that is always available through Jesus.

So Much Joy

You will go out with joy and be led out in peace.
The mountains and hills will burst into song before you,
and all the trees in the fields will clap their hands.

ISAIAH 55:12 NCV

The kingdom of God is not only one of love and peace; it is also full of joy! There is refreshment for the weary soul, reviving of hope for those who have lost sight of theirs, and rivers of pure delight that restore the lightness of life in those who have been beaten down by troubles. As surely as the sun will rise in the east, so will the light of our God lead us forth in peace and bring us out in joy.

Even nature itself will join the chorus of rejoicing that the dark night is over and the light of day has returned. The beauty of creation in its prime is the invitation for us to believe and hope that every season has its end and its inevitable beginning. Flowers will bloom again; new life will spring forth from the earth and the barren branches of naked trees. Though decay will last for a season, there is always new life on the horizon.

Consider how the cycle of seasons relates to your life.

Gardens of Glory

The LORD will guide you always;
he will satisfy your needs in a sun-scorched land
and will strengthen your frame.
You will be like a well-watered garden,
like a spring whose waters never fail.

ISAIAH 58:11 NIV

Wherever you venture in life, know this: you are never alone. The Lord will always be your guide as you look to him. He is the satisfaction your soul craves in every season, and he is your supernatural sustenance in harsh times. He will be your strength as you depend on him. Trust him to do what he has promised to do—to guide you into his goodness.

In the fellowship of the Spirit, you have a never-ending fountain of life, hope, peace, and joy flowing within you. Does your spirit feel dry? Does your soul feel thirsty? Take a moment to close your eyes and tune in to the life already inside your chest. Ask the Spirit to minister to your own spirit with his lifegiving and refreshing waters. Then, you will be like a well-watered garden of his glorious presence.

Commune with the Spirit, thanking God for his waters of refreshment.

Better Word

> "I will give them a crown to replace their ashes,
> and the oil of gladness to replace their sorrow,
> and clothes of praise to replace their spirit of sadness."
>
> ISAIAH 61:3 NCV

Nowhere in the Word does God tell us to ignore our sadness. He does not instruct us to deny the pain and suffering we experience in the tragedies and losses of life. Where did we learn to do this? Why do we use our spirituality to try to bypass what he promised to be with us in? We cannot convince or force ourselves out of grief. We must recognize it, feel it, and move through it in order to heal from it.

Oh, but the wondrous beauty of God's kindness! He says that he will give us a crown of beauty to replace the ashes of our despair. He offers us the oil of his gladness which will seep into our sorrow and turn our mourning into joy. He gives us clothes of praise to replace the spirit of our sadness. We will dance again! We will sing, and we will rise up in the glory of his healing presence. There is hope for the future, and there is peace in our midst for today.

When you feel sad, ask God to minister to you in it.

None Like Him

From ages past no one has heard, no ear has perceived, no eye has seen any God besides you, who works for those who wait for him.

ISAIAH 64:4 NRSV

There is no one like God, who sent his own Son to show us the power of his kingdom ways. In Matthew 5, Jesus lays out the difference between what was understood about the laws of God and what the kingdom of heaven actually requires. But he did not stop there! Knowing that perfection was beyond any of us, he provided a way out from the shame and fear that keep us stuck, and from the power of death itself.

In his death and resurrection, we find our true life. All of us who have come to the Father through Jesus have become like new creations. We are made alive in the tide of his unfailing love that misses nothing. Who else is like this? No one has heard, no eye has seen, no ear has perceived any God besides the Lord who works for those who wait for him.

Trust God with the things you cannot control. Let them go.

Eternal Portion

My flesh and my heart fail;
But God is the strength of my heart
and my portion forever.

PSALM 73:26 NKJV

Even when our bodies fail us and our hearts grow weary in our chests, our souls' strength is still found in the living presence of God. He is the strength of our hearts, and he will always be our perfect portion. This does not mean that we will experience an easy life without flaws or pain. We are not promised a world without trouble, but we are promised the presence of God with us through it all.

May we know the peace of God that transcends our circumstances. May we know his nearness in our frailty and our losses. May we not judge others based on what their bodies are capable of, for that is not where their worth comes from. Instead, let's offer our own bodies as living sacrifices, whatever that looks like for each of us. With no need to judge ourselves, we let the power of God permeate us through and through. He is our hope, our strength, and our deliverer. Let's lean on his wisdom and trust his understanding. He is, after all, our eternally perfect portion.

Instead of judging your body, thank God for it!

Made in Love's Image

Know that the LORD Himself is God;
It is He who has made us, and not we ourselves;
We are His people and the sheep of His pasture.

PSALM 100:3 NASB

We could spend our energy building lives for ourselves and forgetting that we are but one part of a larger whole. We have been made in the image of God, and we were created for community. How do our lives reflect the interconnectedness of creation? Do we give back to our communities, sowing our seeds of generosity into future generations? Or are we living with a smaller scope?

May we dare to look at our lives from the perspective of God, stepping outside of our narrow view of things. His perception is much broader and higher than ours, and yet he doesn't overlook a single detail. We can trust that his wisdom takes everything into account. Are we willing to invite him to challenge the status quo of our lives? Will we yield to his wisdom that speaks challenges to our hearts? May we join with his kingdom values and look from the lens of eternity and not just the right now of our comfort.

Look for ways to serve or bless your local community.

Good and Ready

The Lord is always good and ready to receive you.
He's so loving that it will amaze you—
so kind that it will astound you!
And he is famous for his faithfulness toward all.
Everyone knows our God can be trusted,
for he keeps his promises to every generation!

PSALM 100:5 TPT

What an invitation you have before you today! God, the loving Father of all creation, is good and ready to receive you. Don't let fear of failure hold you back. Don't let the disappointment of your own faults and flaws keep you from him. He is famously faithful to all that he has made. He will not forget a single vow that he has made. He will fulfill every promise; you can count on it.

Come to the Lord today. His love is astoundingly pure. His kindness is unquestionably without rival. He is better than we could ever give him credit for. You can trust him with your heart. He is gentle, and he is reliable. He will not let you go, and he won't ever betray you. He is with you, and his love will never leave you. Turn to him and receive the fullness of his loving kindness once more. Remember, it has no end!

Let the love of God draw you near to his heart.

Gathered In

Do it again, Lord! Save us, O Lord, our God!
Gather us from our exile and unite us together
so that we will give our great
and joyous thanks to you again
and bring you glory by our praises.

PSALM 106:47 TPT

Have you ever felt like a lost cause? Perhaps you have someone in your life that continues to choose cycles of destruction. Does hopelessness fill you when you think of them? Even what seems beyond repair is redeemable and restorable in the great grace of our God. Nothing is impossible for him!

He gathers those who call to him, and he leads them out of their captivity into the freedom of his love. He will do it again. He will restore those who have lost their way. He will lead those who ask for a helping hand. How could we but give joyous thanks when relationships are restored and lost ones are brought back home? May we look to the Lord when we have no other hope, for he will do it again.

Where you are tempted to give up hope,
persevere in prayer.

Story to Tell

Let the redeemed of the LORD tell their story.

PSALM 107:2 NIV

Everyone has a story to tell. Every life is filled with testimonies, and yours is no different. When was the last time you shared an experience that changed you with someone? It does not have to be your whole life story; a piece of it will do. When we share something meaningful from our own lives with others, we often will find ourselves encouraged as well.

Take a few moments to think through your life. What stands out to you? What memories come up? Is there a specific moment in your life that rings through? Perhaps you notice a continual thread that weaves through the different seasons of your life. There is power in your experiences, and there is purpose in your story. Remember who you are. Let how God has moved through your life speak hope over your present circumstances. He is not through with you yet!

Share a portion of your life's story with someone today.

November

All of this is for your benefit.
And as God's grace
reaches more and more people,
there will be great thanksgiving,
and God will receive more and more glory.

2 CORINTHIANS 4:15 NLT

Wholehearted Thanks

Praise the LORD!
I will thank the LORD with all my heart
as I meet with his godly people.

PSALM 111:1 NLT

Are there people in your life that whenever you think of them, your heart swells with gratitude? Supportive family, faithful friendship, and godly community are reflections of God's goodness in our lives. Those people who encourage us when we are struggling, who walk with us through dark valleys of grief, and who celebrate with us in our joyous occasions are gifts from God.

As you consider who these people are in your life, lift up a prayer of praise and thanksgiving to God for each of them. They are an image of his kindness in your life. Consider who you can show up for in the same way. We were created, after all, to do life with others in community and not to depend solely on ourselves. Our greatest gifts in this life are in the form of relationships. May we know this, live this, and give thanks.

Reach out and thank a faithful friend.

Unforgettable Miracles

His unforgettable works of surpassing wonder
reveal his grace and tender mercy.

PSALM 111:4 TPT

There are moments in our lives and in the world that are
unforgettable. Some of memories that will stick with
us, we'd rather forget about. Others are forever marked
because of the communal and societal importance of
them. We remember the time and place we heard the
news. When important occasions happen within our
communities, they become markers in our memories, tragic
or otherwise.

There are unforgettable breakthroughs and miracles that
stick with us, too. What joyous occasions stick out to you?
What miracles have you seen in your lifetime? Don't let
the time and space diminish the joyous impact it had on
you at first. Ask the Lord to refresh your memory, to renew
your courage and hope, and to keep his goodness at the
forefront of your mind.

Share a joyful memory with someone today.

Trustworthy Truth

All he does is just and good,
and all his commandments are trustworthy.

PSALM 111:7 NLT

Everything the Lord does is in line with the truth of his constant character. Everything he has promised, he will do. All that he has revealed himself to be reflects his never-changing nature of loyal love, consistent compassion, and marvelous mercy. When we do not understand why God moves in certain ways, may we look to Jesus for the answers.

Jesus is the living expression of God the Father. He is the fulfillment of the Old Testament law, and he gave clarity and further clues about the kingdom of heaven. The law of his love is the law by which we are to live. Everything he has instructed us to do is with the wisdom of his all-knowing perspective. He asks us to trust him. Do we? May we bind our hearts to his in loyal love, letting his kindness lead us to repentance and into our freedom. He is trustworthy, and every word he speaks is true.

Yield your heart in trust to Jesus and his ways today.

Drenched with Thanksgiving

Return to your rest, my soul,
for the LORD has been good to you.

PSALM 116:7 NIV

In the chaos of our lives, our souls can get caught up in the frenzied pace. In these times, we are not helpless. We can remind ourselves of the peace of God that is available to us here and now. When we are tempted to let worry dictate the confidence of our trust, let's remind our hearts of God's faithful goodness.

We can say with the psalmist, "Return to your rest, my soul." Return to your rest. No matter what has upset the calm and clarity of our hearts, we can speak peace over ourselves. Let's speak to ourselves as we would a good friend, soothing the concerns we have with the truth of who God was, is, and always will be. He is the same faithful, powerful, overcoming God who brings breakthrough. He has not changed, and we can rest assured that his faithfulness is being worked out continually.

Speak peace over the areas of your heart
that are struggling to trust God.

Day of Rejoicing

This is the day which the LORD has made;
Let us rejoice and be glad in it.

PSALM 118:24 NASB

Wherever you find yourself today, in whatever mood, today is the only time you can control. Yesterday is in the past; the future is still out of reach. What can you do with your time, your heart, and your attitude right here and now? Focus on those things.

May you find a reason to rejoice. Maybe it's the simple pleasure of your morning cup of coffee, the way the light filters through your window, or the fresh air that greets your lungs as you step outside. May you find the peace of the presence of the Lord rises up to meet you and also settles your heart. May you find reason after reason to give thanks until it is a steady rhythm that overflows from your soul onto your lips. Think of it as a practice; the more you do it, the more natural it will become.

Look for reasons to give thanks throughout your day.

Revived in Hope

Your promise revives me;
it comforts me in all my troubles.

PSALM 119:50 NLT

There is hope to be found in the promises of the Lord. He is faithful in all he does, so we can trust that what he says he will do, he will follow through on. What promise are you holding onto? What vow of the Lord are you betting your life upon? May it be on the sure foundation of his love above all else. The one who promised is faithful to fulfill it.

Take some time to pray today, inviting the Spirit of peace to settle over your heart and mind as you give him all your worries and cares. He is not slow to answer; his timing is not ours, but it is perfect. Let the comfort of the Lord meet you in the wrestling. May hope rise up within you as he speaks his words of life over you. Fellowship with him. There, in his presence, you will find what you're looking for. Don't hesitate a moment longer!

Take time in prayer and thank God for his faithfulness.

Loving Wisdom

Give thanks to the Creator
who made the heavens with wisdom!
His tender love for us continues on forever!

PSALM 136:5 TPT

The loving wisdom of the Lord guides us through the challenges of this life. When we look to his leadership, we will find his solutions are our portion. Science reflects the wonderful order of God. He is so wise in all that he does! Everything he has created is intricately put together with precision and purpose.

When we are not sure what to do or where to go, let's look to the Lord for his direction. We get to choose which way we will go, but he will give us the discernment we need to make the best choice available. All of his wisdom is loving, so let's not let fear push us in any direction. Where does his kindness guide us? Where does his truth point? Let's build our lives upon the sure foundation of his tried-and-true character. He does not fail!

Look to the Lord for wisdom in your decisions.

Call and Answer

On the day I called you, you answered me.
You made me strong and brave.

PSALM 138:3 NCV

When we call upon the Lord, he answers us. Whatever our need is, he is more than able to meet it. No matter the dilemma, he is capable of directing us through it. He is the light that illuminates the path in front of us. In him there is no darkness, and he sees everything clearly.

Is your heart wavering at the steps you know you must take? Do you need a fresh dose of courage to keep going? Do you need strength to persevere? The Lord your God is with you, and he will not let you go. Be filled with his confidence as you turn to him. With him by your side, you can face and conquer every fear. Trust him as he leads you and continually call out to him. When you need assurance, he will answer you. You just might find he is already closer than you knew.

Take courage in the very present Spirit of God.

Nothing Too Broken

He heals the wounds of every shattered heart.

PSALM 147:3 TPT

In this life, we will all know heartbreak. There is inevitable loss as we grieve those who leave us behind. This is not something we can fix in ourselves, but the healer of every heart can mend the wounds of even the most shattered soul. Nothing is beyond his ability to restore. He can take our tragedies and plant seeds of his mercy in the ashes so that new life will grow out of them.

Does your heart need healing? Is it too much to imagine that God will restore you when you feel so broken? May the peace of God settle over you with the gentle washing of his presence over your being. You are not beyond repair. You are not too far gone. He gives beauty for our ashes, and he will do it for you. Look to him for hope, for he is full of life. He breathes, and we are made alive in him.

Ask God to make all things new in you.
Thank him for his restorative power.

Infinite Understanding

How great is our God!
There's absolutely nothing
his power cannot accomplish,
and he has infinite understanding of everything.

PSALM 147:5 TPT

Whenever we begin to lose our grip on control, that is the beginning of letting go. There is only so much that we can do. We have a limited amount of energy to offer and only so much time in each day to accomplish things. Instead of trying to be superhuman, why don't we let God supernaturally do what only he can? Let's do what we can and leave the rest with him.

God has no limits. There is absolutely nothing that his power cannot accomplish, as the psalmist says. He is not restricted in knowledge as we are. He is not bound to the limits of our humanity. He is so much greater than we can imagine! Let's throw our anchor of hope into the ocean of his mercy and let him lead us, resting in his peace as we sail through this life together.

*Take time at the beginning and end of your day
to give God what you cannot control.*

Time to Sing

Hallelujah! Praise the Lord!
It's time to sing to God a brand-new song
so that all his holy people will hear how wonderful he is!

PSALM 149:1 TPT

Have you ever been so full of joy that others noticed you humming and singing? Perhaps you didn't even realize that you were making melodies, but your good mood automatically turned into song.

God loves it when we offer him brand new songs from our hearts. Why? Because it is a brilliant reflection of what he does over us. Zephaniah 3:17 says that the Lord will "rejoice over you with joyful songs." He is the God who sings joyfully over us! May we offer him the overflow of our gladness and joy in song form. When the praise bubbles up, we can let it out with spontaneous songs that flow from our lips straight to God's heart.

Sing a song of worship to the Lord today—
just between you and him.

Even There

I can never escape from your Spirit!
I can never get away from your presence!
If I ride the wings of the morning,
if I dwell by the farthest oceans,
even there your hand will guide me,
and your strength will support me.

PSALM 139:7, 9-10 NLT

No matter how far we feel like we are from the Lord, we are closer than we could imagine. We cannot escape his Spirit, for he is everywhere. We cannot get away from his presence. His loyal love finds us wherever we are. We are never without it!

In our disappointment, may we not despair. In our heartbreak, may we know that the Lord is near. In the broken dreams that transform our lives forever, may we have clear assurance that even there, God's Spirit meets us with the abundance of his merciful kindness. His strength supports us in every situation. His hand guides us through every murky trial. What a faithful God he is!

Declare the truth of God's presence with you
and look for evidence of his goodness.

As He Was

"I will be with you as I was with Moses.
I will not fail you or abandon you.
Be strong and courageous."

JOSHUA 1:5-6 NLT

The Lord promises to be with those who look to him for help. When we trust in him, yielding our lives to his love, we can be sure that he will come through. Let us take our confidence from his words to Joshua, for his promise to us in Christ is the same today.

"I will be with you as I was with Moses." Moses led the Israelites out of their captivity in Egypt, and the Lord did miraculous signs and wonders through him. The Spirit within us is the same power that moved with Moses and the same power that moved through Christ. "I will not fail you or abandon you." He promises to never leave us, and he will be faithful to his vows. "Be strong and courageous." No matter what you are dealing with or walking into today, know that the Lord your God goes with you.

*When you are overwhelmed, remember
that God is with you.*

Our Liberator

"Let us praise the Lord, the God of Israel, because he has come to help his people and has given them freedom. He has given us a powerful Savior."

LUKE 1:68-69 NCV

Thank God that we are seen, known, and understood by a gracious father! He has provided everything that we need for freedom in this life—freedom of the soul, no matter our circumstances. He has given us full access to his love, to his kingdom, and to himself through Christ, his Son.

Whatever is holding you back, whatever is keeping you stuck, whatever is pushing you down today, know that there is freedom for you in Christ. His love liberates us from our bondage. Where sin, shame, and fear keep us small and enclosed, his mercy sets us in open spaces of possibility. Look to him today for all that you need. Rejoice in his love; it is your liberation.

Give Jesus the areas where you just can't seem to make progress. Receive the power of his liberating love.

Light of Breakthrough

"Because of God's tender mercy,
the morning light from heaven
is about to break upon us,
to give light to those who sit in darkness
and in the shadow of death,
to guide us to the path of peace."

LUKE 1:78-79 NLT

No matter how dark the season of night we are in, there is always a path of peace that leads us into the breaking light of day. Our breakthrough is coming! May we take hope and take heart in the words of Zechariah's prophecy in Luke. He was talking about Jesus. He is the Light of the world, and in his light, we find life.

In the darkness of our suffering, the light of Christ shines through. There is absolutely nothing that his love does not light up. There are no shadows in his peace. He is the peace of God. He is the liberator of our souls. He is our breakthrough in every circumstance. He is Jesus, and he is always available.

Remember that Jesus is the path of peace to God and look to him today.

Molded with Purpose

"You guided my conception and formed me in the womb. You clothed me with skin and flesh, and you knit my bones and sinews together."

JOB 10:10-11 NLT

It is a deep comfort to know that we are intimately known by the Creator of the universe. Not only did he put us together, but he knows what makes us tick. He sees the motivations of our hearts, senses the pull of our desires, and understands the paths we take. We are known on the deepest level imaginable. And not only that, but we are loved more fully than we can comprehend.

When we are lacking in purpose, may we go to the one who knit us together in the first place. He knows us best. When we are confused about what path to take, let's look to the Lord for clarity, for he understands us better than we know ourselves. We were not created to go off on our own. We were made for relationship with our Maker. May we deepen our fellowship, knowing that in his love, we come alive to who we were always made to be.

Spend time with the Lord and ask him for fresh understanding of how he made you.

Don't Forget

Bless the LORD, O my soul,
and all that is within me,
bless his holy name!
Bless the LORD, O my soul,
and forget not all his benefits.

PSALM 103:1-2 ESV

In the stresses of life, we can get too busy to make time for quiet moments with the Lord. If we're not paying attention, the burdens of our days may weigh us down gradually until we have a sense of hopelessness in the overwhelm of life's demands. Have we forgotten the benefits of knowing the Lord?

In his presence, there is peace. In his presence, there is fullness of joy. In his presence, there is full acceptance in the loving tide of his affection. In his presence, we find purpose. In his presence, no topic is off limits. In his presence, we trade our heavy burdens for his light load. In his presence, we partner with the Living God. In his presence, we are made new over and over again. Today, let's spend time in his presence.

Take time to worship the Lord.

Compassionate Father

The LORD is like a father to his children,
tender and compassionate to those who fear him.
For he knows how weak we are;
he remembers we are only dust.

PSALM 103:13-14 NLT

Whatever our relationship with our earthly fathers, we have a kind and compassionate Father in heaven. He is the King of kings, the Creator of the universe, and Lord above all. Still, he makes time for us whenever we turn to him. His attention span is not limited; it is infinite.

May we never make excuses for why we should not bother him with our dilemmas. He is a wonderful Father who takes time for his children. He gives us advice through his wonderful wisdom. He offers us comfort in our pain, no matter how small it may seem to us. He welcomes us with open arms that draw us in with kindness. He delights in our fellowship. He loves it when we come to him! He is a father who rises up on behalf of his children, and he gives us the freedom to choose our way. He is so much better than we can imagine. Let's leave every excuse we can think of at the door and run into his open arms today.

When you see someone acting in compassion today, thank them for it.

So Close

God you are near me always, so close to me;
every one of your commands reveals truth.
I've known all along how true and unchanging
is every word you speak, established forever!

PSALM 119:151-152 TPT

Have you known the closeness of the Lord that the psalmist describes in this beautiful poem? Does it resonate in your heart, echoing how you feel about your relationship with God? Perhaps, it leaves you a little hungry, like you want to believe that he is near, but you just aren't sure.

It is never too late to grow in your relationship with the Lord. He is a close friend, there whenever you need him. Perhaps you have not known his closeness but find yourself desiring it. Whether or not you've experienced the confidence of his closeness on a regular basis in your life, you can cultivate deeper relationship with the Spirit of God who is with you. Ask for a greater awareness of his presence in your life. God rewards hunger with satisfaction. Ask and you will receive.

Thank God for his presence with you and press in
for deeper revelation of his nearness.

Revelation Light

In the middle of the night I awake to give thanks to you
because of all your revelation-light; so right and true!

PSALM 119:62 TPT

There is an endless storehouse of wisdom in the kingdom
of God. Even the most astute minds in the world have not
reached the breadth of his understanding. Not even close!
May we approach this life as learners of God's kingdom
culture. May we take every opportunity to ask him for more
understanding of his ways. He gives revelation-light, as
today's verse says, and we can perceive parts of him that
we did not know before.

The wisdom of God, as in all things in the Lord, is
expansive. So is his mercy, his justice, his kindness, and so
on. We cannot comprehend the vastness of God's being in
our limited perspectives where everything has boundaries
and limits. With God, there are no restrictions. Nothing can
hold him. May we rise up to meet him in the expanse of
his perspective, and may we reject the idea that he can be
contained.

Ask God for greater revelation of his limitlessness.

Tides of Goodness

Everything you do is beautiful,
flowing from your goodness;
teach me the power of your wonderful words!

PSALM 119:68 TPT

When we aren't sure what God is up to in the midst of
our messes, may we turn our attention to his unchanging
character. He is merciful—that we know. He is full of
compassion. He gives grace away like a candy-thrower at
a parade, except with an unending source that covers us
continually. He is a good father, caring for his children. He
is a master restorer, redeemer, and all-around faithful God.
There is no one else like him!

When we are tempted to reduce God down to the limits of
our circumstances, may we be challenged to look higher,
wider, deeper, and longer. There, we will find that his
loving kindness has no end. There are no boundaries to his
power, and there is nothing that is not motivated by the
overwhelming love of his being. He is good, and everything
he does is beautiful. If the fruit is not beautiful, then it's
probably not God's.

*Measure the fruit of your life by God's standards,
not the world's.*

Instruction in Suffering

My suffering was good for me,
for it taught me to pay attention to your decrees.

PSALM 119:71 NLT

None of us would admit to loving suffering. Pain is not the highlight of our lives. But even in suffering, good fruit can grow. In the soil of suffering, where our tears water the seeds of our dreams, the fruit of endurance and hope will break through.

When we go through times of distress, our perspectives become clearer. All of a sudden, we realize what truly matters to us. We become more focused and better able to say no to the things that do not serve our seasons well. When we are struggling, we are much more open to the help and wisdom of those we trust. When we trust in the Lord, we turn to him for help. He becomes a support for us, comforting us in ways that no one else can. So, even though we do not love suffering, let us remember that there is goodness that grows even there, for God is with us.

List three things that suffering has taught you about yourself and about God.

All Parts Matter

If the whole body were an eye, it would not be able to hear... If each part of the body were the same part, there would be no body. But truly God put all the parts, each one of them, in the body as he wanted them.

1 Corinthians 12:17-18 NCV

As humans, we are so prone to comparison. We may look at the lives of those we admire and think that they have the better end of the stick. We may strive to become like them, emulating their style choices, parenting styles, and diets. Perhaps we want their success, their joy, or their family dynamic. It's important for us to look at our lives through the lens of thanksgiving, remembering that what we have may be what someone else longs for.

We were not created to be carbon copies of one another. We were not meant for sameness. That doesn't equal safety or greatness; it is simply familiarity. May we reach beyond the pull of comparison to dig deep into what God has created us to be, right here and now. Instead of trying to shrink or rise to another's standard, let's be free in God's standard. Let's stop comparing and start living in the liberty of love.

Write down ten things you are grateful for in your present life.

Confident Help

I look up to the hills,
but where does my help come from?
My help comes from the Lord,
who made heaven and earth.

Psalm 121:1-2 ncv

When the psalmist wrote, "I look up to the hills, but where does my help come from," he was introducing a necessary perspective shift. He was looking to the hills around him for soldiers to come running over them. He was looking for men when he needed to be looking to God. He realized that his true help and protection could only come from the Lord.

Are you looking at the hills, wondering when help will arrive? Are you surrounded and feeling completely vulnerable to attack? Instead of frantically looking around, look instead to your Creator, the Maker of heaven and earth. He does not sleep or slumber, and he has not lost track of you. He is your true help, and he will keep you safe in the shelter of his presence. He will not let you be overcome by fear. Look to him!

Pray to the Lord when you are overcome by worry.
Thank him for his help.

Keeper of the Watch

The LORD keeps you from all harm
and watches over your life.
The LORD keeps watch over you as you come and go,
both now and forever.

PSALM 121:7-8 NLT

We cannot be alert at all times. We grow tired, and we need sleep. We need to rely on others to keep watch for us when we cannot. When we are vulnerable, we must depend on the help of those around us to keep us safe. In the same way, we rely on God to keep watch over us. He never tires, and his attention doesn't wander. He sees everything at all times. Nothing escapes his notice.

We can trust God to watch over our coming and our going. We can trust him to watch over every area of our lives. We might be surprised, but he never is. Though we may jump to worst case scenarios, he is always with us in the midst of our trials and troubles. When we are weak, he is still strong.

When you see someone in need, offer a helping hand.

Guarded by God

He will keep you from every form of evil or calamity
as he continually watches over you.
You will be guarded by God himself.
You will be safe when you leave your home
and safely you will return.
He will protect you now,
and he'll protect you forevermore!

PSALM 121:7-8 TPT

The Lord is our guardian. He keeps us safe, protecting us
from the attacks of enemy forces. He gives us insight into
our problems, and he rises up in our defense when we
are left out in the open. God himself wraps around us as a
shield. He is our peace. He is our shelter. He is the keeper
of our souls.

Can you remember a time when it seemed as if all odds
were against you and you were going to be overtaken by
tragedy? Can you recall a moment when you were sure
it was going to go one way, and you were relieved to
see it went differently? God's protection over our lives is
consistent. May we look to him and praise him for how he
has kept us along the way.

Thank God for his protection over your life.

Wonderfully Made

You created my inmost being;
you knit me together in my mother's womb.
I praise you because I am fearfully
and wonderfully made;
your works are wonderful,
I know that full well.

PSALM 139:13-14 NIV

Think about someone you love dearly. Consider what it is that delights you about who they are. Think of their personality traits, the curve of their smile, and the infectiousness of their laugh. Now, consider this; the Lord delights in you in even greater measure!

When we put our time into creating something meaningful, it gets our energy, our time, and our sacrifice. It demands our attention and our care. Perhaps as it takes shape, we begin to change our perception of the work of our hands. What was once a project becomes a passion. God is a masterful creator and artist. Everything he has made has his fingerprints all over it. May we see ourselves through the pride of his eyes today.

Reach out to someone you love and tell them what a delight it is to know them.

He Sees It All

You discern my going out and my lying down;
you are familiar with all my ways.
Before a word is on my tongue,
you, Lord, know it completely.
You hem me in behind and before,
and you lay your hand upon me.

PSALM 139:3-5 NIV

Nothing in our lives is a mystery to God. We cannot hide our habits or our quirks from him. He is familiar with every single one of our ways. Knowing that he is a loving and faithful father, this should comfort us. He does not demean us even in our failures and mistakes. He loves us to life with the kindness in his correction. He always builds us up. He does not tear us down.

May we give God our complete trust and hope, knowing that he does not miss a single detail of our hopes, dreams, and hard work. He sees it all. He knows our hearts through and through. He hems us in behind and before, going with us into every trial and every triumph. He sees what grieves our hearts, and he knows what brings us joy. Let us share in his fellowship in every moment as we walk with him through this life.

Thank God for his consistent presence and love.

Constant Meditation

Generation after generation
will declare more of your greatness,
And discover more of your glory.
Your magnificent splendor
And the miracles of your majesty
Are my constant meditation.
Your awe-inspiring acts of power have everyone talking!
And I'm telling people everywhere
about your excellent greatness!

PSALM 145:4-6 TPT

The kingdom of God is always expanding. Each generation tastes the goodness of God as he reveals himself to them in faithfulness. Today, we are building on a foundation of generations that have tasted and seen the glory of God. What was their ceiling has become our floor. Our starting point is a higher place because of what God has already revealed to and through them.

May we look for the miracles of his majesty, constantly meditating on the wonders of our glorious God and King. Jesus, our Redeemer, is the living expression of the Father. We can know God more fully because Jesus revealed him to us. May we look for the evidence of the fruit of the Spirit in and around us, the excellent greatness of our God in our lives.

Tell someone what God has done for you.

The Lord Reigns

Tremble before Him, all the earth.
The world also is firmly established,
It shall not be moved. Let the heavens rejoice,
and let the earth be glad; and let them say
among the nations, "The Lord reigns."

1 Chronicles 16:30-31 nkjv

The Lord is powerful, sovereign, and good. His glory is beyond our understanding. Think of the most beautiful sunrise you've ever witnessed. Conjure up images of the most stunning vista you've ever seen. The glory and beauty of the Lord is immeasurably greater!

One day, when Jesus returns and all wrong things are made right, we will be ushered into the coming age of his reign. We will see him in all his glory, and the fullness of his majesty will be before us. He will shine brighter than the sun. There will be no shadow or hidden thing. Everything will be made clear. We will know him fully, even as we are fully known by him.

Watch the sun rise or set soon
and remember how sovereign God is.

December

You have taken away my clothes of mourning
and clothed me with joy,
that I might sing praises to you
and not be silent.
O Lᴏʀᴅ my God,
I will give you thanks forever!

Psᴀʟᴍ 30:11-12 ɴʟᴛ

Eyes Fixed

I keep my eyes always on the LORD.
With him at my right hand, I will not be shaken.
Therefore my heart is glad and my tongue rejoices;
my body also will rest secure.

PSALM 16:8-9 NIV

When we keep our attention fixed on the Lord, our hearts rest in the peace and confidence of his power and presence. When our eyes are set on our Savior, we are given greater perspective than we can achieve on our own. His understanding is higher than ours, after all! No matter the challenges ahead, the busyness of our schedules, or the demands on our time, may we keep our eyes fixed on our good, good God.

He is our center. He is our solid ground. When we set our lives in the orbit of his love, everything falls into place. Our hearts align in his presence. Our service reflects his kingdom. Let's remember him as our purpose and motivation. Let's never forget to look to him, for he is constant in mercy and faithful in loyal love. In him, we will find rest for our souls.

Start and end your day by looking to Jesus.

Rich Soil

Blessed is the man who trusts in the LORD,
And whose hope is the LORD.
For he shall be like a tree planted by the waters,
Which spreads out its roots by the river,
And will not fear when heat comes;
But its leaf will be green,
And will not be anxious in the year of drought,
Nor will cease from yielding fruit.

JEREMIAH 17:7-8 NKJV

When our trust is rooted in the rich soil of God's faithfulness, we will know the constant peace of God. Even when storms come, we will remain firmly established. Even when spiritual droughts enter our lives, we will still produce the fruit of his Spirit in our lives. There is no need to fear when perfect love is our sustenance and source.

May we place our hope in the unfailing mercy of the Lord. He meets us with his lavish love every time we turn to him. Though we have trials and troubles in this life, we have the constant help of God. He is a sure and steady place of refuge. Let's keep looking to him through every season of the soul. No matter what we face, he is all-powerful, almighty, all-knowing, and full of loyal love for his children.

Choose to trust God with your worries today.

Shielded by God

God's way is perfect.
All the LORD's promises prove true.
He is a shield for all who look to him for protection.
For who is God except the LORD?
Who but our God is a solid rock?

PSALM 18:30-31 NLT

Has hope felt like a commodity you just can't grab a hold of? Does it feel as if the peace of God is elusive? With so much trouble in the world around us and a constant barrage of bad news streaming from various sources, we can forget to look for the good news. When the world has us down, let's remember that there is more at work than meets the eye.

We know through God's Word that the Lord is with us. We know that he has promised to wipe every tear from every eye when he ushers in his eternal kingdom. The hope we have to look forward to may feel out of reach, but his presence is ever so close. He is a shield for those who look to him, and he will not go back on his word.

Be someone's safe space today.

Great Joy

The angel said to them, "Do not be afraid. I bring you good news that will cause great joy for all the people. Today in the town of David a Savior has been born to you; he is the Messiah, the Lord."

LUKE 2:10-11 NIV

As we approach the celebration of the first coming of Jesus, let our hearts be tender to the good news of his life. When we look at the humanity of Jesus' arrival, the beginning of his life could not have been more humble. He was born into a normal and struggling family as they went to Bethlehem to register for the census, and he was born in a room filled with animals.

In this humble introduction to life, Jesus was as dependent on his parents as any vulnerable newborn. As he grew and matured, he also grew in wisdom. He was a normal boy with a normal upbringing, yet he was the Savior of the world. What great news! This boy-turned-man would be the hope of every longing soul. And so he is. The Messiah has come, and he has brought peace between God and humankind. Praise the Lord!

Read about Jesus' youth through the lens of his humanity.

Many Nations

"Sing and rejoice, O daughter of Zion! For behold, I am coming and I will dwell in your midst," says the LORD. "Many nations shall be joined to the LORD in that day, and they shall become My people. And I will dwell in your midst. Then you will know that the LORD of hosts has sent Me to you."

ZECHARIAH 2:10-11 NKJV

The prophetic declaration in this passage from Zechariah foreshadows the coming of Jesus. He was the one who came to join the nations to the Lord. He has made a way for every nation, tribe, family, and soul to come to the Father. He is the path to fullness of fellowship with God as the bridge we needed, and he has eliminated every obstacle that stood in the way.

May we run into the presence of the Lord by his Spirit. He dwells with us even now as we wait for his second coming. His Spirit is our assurance, our holy help, and the empowering presence of God to live as overcomers in this world. The Spirit dwells with all those who call on the name of Jesus, no matter what language. He is not only found in our familiar traditions; he is so much greater than that. May we sing and rejoice as we recognize the Spirit's work in the far reaches of the world.

Talk to someone from a different culture than yours.

Spiritual Seasons

"Arise, my love, my beautiful one,
and come away,
for behold, the winter is past;
the rain is over and gone.
The flowers appear on the earth,
the time of singing has come."

SONG OF SOLOMON 2:10-12 ESV

Spiritual seasons work in cycles just as the seasons of earth do. They do not follow the same timeline, though. What sort of season do you find yourself in? Have you just entered the hopeful new life of a spiritual spring? You will know it by the hope that sings in your heart and fills the air around you. Does a fruitful summer better suit where you are, with long days full of joy and fellowship?

Are you in the harvest season of fall? You may recognize that you are reaping the reward of work you put in during previous seasons. Or do you find yourself in a barren winter, where the cold has driven you to crave small gatherings with close friends? There is no right or wrong season to be in. As you recognize the present term you're in, may you find encouragement in knowing that there is purpose in it.

Thank God for the spiritual season you are in.

Gracious Living

The grace of God has appeared that offers salvation to all people. It teaches us to say "No" to ungodliness and worldly passions, and to live self-controlled, upright and Godly lives in this present age.

TITUS 2:11-12 NIV

What does it look like to live a gracious life? When we align our lives with the kingdom of our God, we make his love our standard in all things. The way we live in our day-to-day matters. We do not live to simply please ourselves, for those rewards are fleeting. When we submit our lives to Christ, living for his kingdom come and his will being done on the earth, our habits and priorities will reflect it.

To live upright and godly lives is to submit our desires to the desires of the Lord. He always knows what is best for us. His wisdom takes our humanity into account. He does not require anything of us that he does not empower us to do. Let us look to the life of Jesus, to his words and his actions, and follow him on the path of his love. We do not sacrifice anything that he has not already sacrificed.

Say no to temptation today; practice self-control.

Rescued

My heart rejoices in the LORD!
The Lord has made me strong.
Now I have an answer for my enemies;
I rejoice because you rescued me.
No one is holy like the LORD!
There is no one besides you;
there is no Rock like our God.

1 SAMUEL 2:1-2 NLT

The Lord rescues us and sets us on the solid rock of his unshakable mercy. He has already done it through the resurrection power of Jesus. There is nothing in this life that lies outside the power of his life. He is the holy and perfect Lamb of God. We have been rescued from the dominion of sin and from the powers of fear and shame that kept us in cycles that would not quit.

In the overwhelming love of God, we have found our purpose. We come alive in the abundance of his life within us. He causes our hearts to rejoice and our spirits to sing, for he is our strength in every trial. There is nothing that he has not already overcome through the power of his sacrifice. There is nothing that does not come under the authority of his blood when we give our lives to him. Let us rejoice in the freedom he has given us. Let us lean on our rescuer in all things.

Sing a song of praise to the Lord.

Pray for All People

Pray for all people. Ask God for the things people need, and be thankful to him. You should pray for kings and for all who have authority. Pray for the leaders so that we can have quiet and peaceful lives—lives full of worship and respect for God.

1 Timothy 2:1-2 NLT

Prayer is a practice. It is not reserved for those who are super holy. It is the way that we communicate with God, and it is a lifeline for us in all things. May we pray without ceasing, leaving an open line of communication throughout the day, coming back to him again and again. As we pray, we also invite the Lord to speak to us. He wants a dialogue, not a monologue.

There is absolutely nothing off limits when it comes to prayer. It is how we develop a deeper relationship with the Lord. Where we have hesitated to bring things to the Lord, may we let the walls of reluctance crumble. As we pray for all people, his compassion within us will grow. As we lift up situations to him, he may offer us insight and solutions. Let us open our hearts and our prayer lives to God in broader ways today.

Pray for the needs of others to be met and pray for our leaders in the government.

God's Dwelling

God's dwelling place is now among the people, and he
will dwell with them. "He will wipe every tear from their
eyes. There will be no more death" or mourning or crying
or pain, for the old order of things has passed away.

REVELATION 21:3-4 NIV

What a wonderful hope we have to look forward to when
Christ returns and ushers in the coming age of his kingdom
reign. We have a taste of his leadership through fellowship
with his Spirit here and now; that is certain. But when Jesus
makes his physical dwelling with us, and us with him, every
mystery will be laid to rest in the clarity of his gloriously
unfiltered presence.

He will wipe every tear from our eyes. There will be no
more mourning, for separation and loss will be but a
memory. When the new order of his kingdom is put in
place, there will be fullness of joy, of peace, and of love.
Every hope will be fulfilled in him. Everything we do not
yet know will be known. Everything we long for still will be
satisfied. What a glorious day and age to look forward to!

*Thank God for his coming kingdom
and for the fullness of hope that awaits you.*

Oasis of Peace

The Lord is my best friend and my shepherd.
I always have more than enough.
He offers a resting place for me in his luxurious love.
His tracks take me to an oasis of peace,
the quiet brook of bliss.

PSALM 23:1-2 TPT

When we find our hearts are heavy, let us turn to our Shepherd and best friend. Jesus is the Good Shepherd, always leading us in the pathways of his peace and love. Even when we pass through valleys, he guides in his kindness. In him, there is more than enough for all that we need. He is our source, and he is the wisest leader and most trusted confidant we will ever know.

Today, if we are weighed down by the worries of unknowns looming before us, may we follow the Lord to his resting place. There, luxurious love restores and revives us. He leads us to a peaceful oasis where we can be refreshed in the brook of his bliss. He truly is better than we can imagine. There is nothing that he leaves out. Let's lay down our burdens and rest awhile in his presence.

Turn off your notifications and spend several minutes in silence, doing nothing.

Heaven and Earth

"I am a God who is near," says the LORD.
"I am also a God who is far away.
No one can hide where I cannot see him," says the LORD.
"I fill all of heaven and earth," says the LORD.

JEREMIAH 23:23-24 NCV

The Lord's greatness is beyond comprehension. He fills the universe, and yet it cannot hold him. He is everywhere by his Spirit, and yet he cannot be contained by our boundaries and limitations. He is so much greater than our understanding can hold. Even our wildest imaginings of his vast power cannot compare to the immensity of his being.

May we put every problem up against the matchless power of God. May we dare to imagine that God is as good as he says he is, as thoroughly available as he promises, and as mighty as his resurrection life indicates. There is nowhere we could hide from him, for he fills all of heaven and earth. There is no need to hide, for he meets us with his vast tide of mercy. He is holy, he is righteous, and he will make all wrong things right.

Look to the sky when you pray today,
remembering how infinite God is.

How Wonderful

I come to your altar, O LORD,
singing a song of thanksgiving
and telling of all your wonders.

PSALM 26:6-7 NLT

The wonders of God bring us to a place of worship. When we consider the work of his hands and what he has done in our lives and relationships, how could we but thank him? His restorative and redemptive power makes everything new, and we catch glimpses of his goodness as his mercy meets us in the details of our lives.

How wonderful it is that he loves us! How wondrous that he dwells with us through his Spirit. How glorious that we can know and worship him in spirit and in truth. Let everything that has breath, including you, praise the Lord. Let's praise him for the good that he's done. Let's praise him for the way he works his redemption through our lives. There is nothing and no one too far-gone. He is our hope, our strength, and the fullness of life.

Write a poem of thanks to God for what he has done.

Wholehearted Devotion

"You will call on me and come and pray to me,
and I will listen to you.
You will seek me and find me
when you seek me with all your heart."

JEREMIAH 29:12-13 NIV

What holds you back from coming to God? What keeps you from praying? Do you have questions, doubts, or disappointments? Bring them along! Instead of letting them build a barrier between you and God, bring them as an offering. Hand them to him, come to him continually, and pray to him whenever you think of it.

It is not foolish to rely on God's help, and it is not irresponsible to ask for his wisdom. Let's seek him even in our questioning. Let's look for him and turn to him in prayer even in the wrestling. He welcomes our questions. We don't have to have it all figured out or know what we believe about every theological concept. Let's simply press into knowing him more.

Offer God the honesty of your hesitations.

Sojourners

"Who am I and who are my people that we should be able to offer as generously as this? For all things come from You, and from Your hand we have given You. For we are sojourners before You, and tenants, as all our fathers were; our days on the earth are like a shadow, and there is no hope."

1 CHRONICLES 29:14-15 NASB

Life is fleeting. When we realize how limited our time on earth is, we become aware of the importance of how we spend it. We are not building kingdoms for ourselves. Even if we were, they would not last. May we have the clarity of mind and the sobriety of heart to consider that today is all we have. Though we may build toward the future, let's make sure the kingdom of God is our ultimate vision.

We are travelers in this life, only here for a short time. May we not spend on our energies, time, resources, and attention on fleeting things that will not matter in the end. Let's give ourselves to loving God, loving each other, and extending the values of God's kingdom wherever and whenever we have the chance.

Write down what you want to be remembered for.

In Your Midst

The LORD has taken away the judgments against you; he
has cleared away your enemies. The King of Israel, the
LORD, is in your midst; you shall never again fear evil. On
that day it shall be said to Jerusalem: "Fear not, O Zion;
let not your hands grow weak."

ZEPHANIAH 3:15-16 ESV

Do we live like the Lord is in our midst? In the
conversations we have with our friends, coworkers, and
family, do we reflect that God is with us? How about in how
we treat servers, customer service representatives, and
others? The Lord does not ridicule or shame others. May
we not excuse this behavior in ourselves.

Let's aim to live as those who reflect the mercy of Christ,
extending love to others even when they are hurling
judgments. May we strive to be kind, especially to those
who often don't receive such kindness from strangers. Let's
practice patience, knowing that the Spirit of God is patient
with us. Let's build endurance in our relationships, seeking
restoration rather than arguing over unchangeable things.
Let's be promoters of peace just as God is. In all things,
let's remember that he is with us and live like it.

*Thank God for his Spirit who empowers you
to choose his ways over your own.*

Yet I Will

Even though the fig trees have no blossoms,
and there are no grapes on the vines;
even though the olive crop fails,
and the fields lie empty and barren;
even though the flocks die in the fields,
and the cattle barns are empty,
yet I will rejoice in the LORD!
I will be joyful in the God of my salvation!

HABAKKUK 3:17-18 NLT

In the barren times of our lives, how do we approach God? Is it with the confidence that he is still good, even if our circumstances and experiences don't line up in the moment? There is so much to give thanks to God for in our harvest and abundance. It is easy to praise God when things are going well for us.

But what about when things are hard? When we lose jobs, our relationships fail, and tragedy strikes? What then? Can we still find reasons to praise him? Can we still believe that he is good? He remains the God of our salvation, and he has not left us. May we find reason to rejoice in the Lord, even in our barrenness.

Rejoice in the presence of the Lord today.

Never-ending Mercy

I have hope when I think of this:
The LORD's love never ends;
his mercies never stop.
They are new every morning.

LAMENTATIONS 3:21-23 NCV

No matter what we are facing—disappointments, discouragement, trials, or extreme circumstances—may we find our hope in the same place that the author of Lamentations did. Let's meditate on the beautiful truth that God's love never ends. Never, ever. There's no lack in his love. His mercies will never end. We will never reach the end of them because they are new every morning.

Like freshly baked bread, God's mercies are offered fresh every morning. He doesn't give us stale advice or make us live off of yesterday's portion. There is an abundance of mercy in his heart, and he has more than enough to feed us for the rest of our days into the eternity of his kingdom. There is more than enough available to us right here and now to revive, refresh, console, and restore us.

Meditate on the enormity of God's mercy today.

Depend on Him

The LORD is good to those who depend on him,
to those who search for him.
So it is good to wait quietly
for salvation from the LORD.

LAMENTATIONS 3:25-26 NLT

Those who depend on the Lord will not be put to shame.
They will not be disappointed, for God always comes
through, and his promises will all be fulfilled. May we learn
to wait on the Lord. May we grow in being able to slow
down and patiently wait for God to speak to us. He will
show us the way; he will not leave us.

Whenever we are confronted by troubles or questions
that we do not have an answer for, let's remember to look
to the Lord. Let's go to him in prayer, wait on his Spirit
to move within us, and wait for him to speak his words
of wisdom to our hearts. When we look for the Lord and
depend on his help, we will find satisfaction in his power.
He is so very good to those who rely on him.

Spend time waiting on the Lord, listening for his voice.

Sustained

I lie down and sleep;
I wake again, because the LORD sustains me.

PSALM 3:3-4 NIV

What a blessing it is that we don't need to strive to earn God's favor. We come to the Father through Christ, and in him we find full acceptance and love as we yield our hearts to him. The Spirit fills us with the peace of God, which settles our anxious thoughts and calms our worried hearts.

Rest is spiritual. It is holy. After God created the heavens, the earth, and everything in them, he took a day to rest. Jesus took time away to rest. We, too, need sleep. We need to be able to enjoy our lives and not just work all the time. May we make rest a priority, taking what time we can to simply take pleasure in simple things and restore our souls without the demands of responsibility weighing upon us. Let's put down the to-do lists regularly and build rhythms of rest into our schedules.

Thank God for restful sleep.

Living Prayer

Let joy be your continual feast. Make your life a prayer.
And in the midst of everything be always giving thanks,
for this is God's perfect plan for you in Christ Jesus.

1 Thessalonians 5:16-18 TPT

When you think of prayer, what comes to mind? Is it a
quiet place in your home where you spend time with the
Lord? Is it a place of worship where you pray with others?
Is it in nature, where your soul is moved by creation? Is it a
breath, a word, or a stream of consciousness?

Paul says in Thessalonians that we should make our lives
a prayer. That includes everything we do, the sum of our
choices, actions, and interactions. Prayer is more than
words, more than an attitude of the heart. It is a lifestyle.
With that in mind, how can you develop yourself into a
living prayer? In the midst of everything, keep your heart
open to the Lord, letting your thanks pour out and his truth
pour in. Let it all be the give and take of living relationship.

Offer your choices, habits, words, and work
as prayer to God today.

Lifegiving Fruit

The fruit of the Spirit is love, joy, peace, patience, kindness, goodness, faithfulness, gentleness, self-control; against such things there is no law.

GALATIANS 5:22-23 ESV

There is no law against the fruit of the Spirit because they are all reflective of God's nature. Think about it in this way: what legal reason could a person have to prosecute someone because they followed through on their word? What standing would someone have against another person's patience? How could joy be outlawed?

When we look at the fruit of the Spirit, it is plain to see that one would be hard-pressed to indict someone based on any of it. That is true in our society, but how much more in the kingdom of God? There is so much liberty in the law of love. It is what Christ talked about, and it is the precedent we are to model in our lives. Let's live according to the ways of God's kingdom. When we do, his spiritual fruit will be evident in our lives.

Practice one of the fruits of the Spirit consciously throughout your day.

Dance of Joy

David danced with all his might before the LORD. He had on a holy linen vest. David and all the Israelites shouted with joy and blew the trumpets as they brought the Ark of the LORD to the city.

2 SAMUEL 6:14-15 NCV

David danced with all of his might before the Lord, not caring what others thought of him. He, the king of Israel, was basically dancing in the streets in his underwear! It doesn't get much more undignified than that. He didn't let the propriety of others keep him from expressing his joy before the Lord.

Do we let the opinions of others affect our freedom and joy? This is not to say we need to wear next to nothing and dance in the street in the name of God. But in what areas do we keep ourselves from fully expressing our joy when we feel it? May we rejoice in the Lord, knowing that he loves our offerings even when they may seem silly to others. Let's shake off the shame and be free before the Lord in our expressions of joy in worship.

Dance before the Lord.

Sacred Rest

The apostles returned to Jesus from their ministry tour and told him all they had done and taught. Then Jesus said, "Let's go off by ourselves to a quiet place and rest awhile." He said this because there were so many people coming and going that Jesus and his apostles didn't even have time to eat.

MARK 6:30-31 NLT

Now is the perfect time to retreat from the crowds of shopping malls and big holiday gatherings to rest and reflect with those closest to us. Jesus suggested a retreat from the overwhelming crowds to his disciples, and they went off to find a quiet place to rest awhile. In the same way, let us give up the need to perform and allow ourselves time to rest with those we love.

Jesus knows our limits, and he also celebrates our victories with us. Instead of sending his disciples back out after their ministry tour, he invited them to take a break with him. Let's follow his example and take a well-deserved break. We are nearing the end of a busy year, and it is time to recoup.

Spend time at home relaxing with your loved ones.

All We Need

To the fatherless he is a father.
To the widow he is a champion friend.
To the lonely he makes them part of a family.
To the prisoners he leads into prosperity
until they sing for joy.

PSALM 68:5-6 TPT

In Jesus, we truly find all that we need. God is a father to the fatherless. He is a champion friend to the widow. He sets the lonely in family. He leads prisoners into prosperity. It's what he's all about! The liberty of his love is available to us all right where we are. There is no need to go searching for his mercy; it always meets us.

Whatever you need today, may you find it in the presence of God with you. Jesus is Emmanuel, God with us. He came to seek and save the lost. He came to heal and reclaim the broken. He came to set the record straight about the overwhelming love of the Father. He came to provide unhindered access to God. He is the one who breaks every barrier. He has already done it. Let's look to him and find all that our hearts long for. He is all-sufficient for us!

Reach out to someone you know is lonely today.

Whatever We Do

"Ask all the people of the land and the priests, 'When you fasted and mourned in the fifth and seventh months for the past seventy years, was it really for me that you fasted? And when you were eating and drinking, were you not just feasting for yourselves?"

ZECHARIAH 7:4-7 NIV

When we do something in the name of tradition, of church, and of Spirit, let's be sure that the intentions of our hearts are actually in line with God's values. When we fast, let us fast unto the Lord. When we feast, let's do it with thanks to the Lord for the bounty we receive. When we sing, let's do it from hearts that overflow with praise. When we pray, let's look to God and not to what others think of us.

In all things, may our hearts be submitted to the Father. His ways are higher than our ways. Do we just go through the motions of our rituals and rites, not thinking about the meaning? Have we become so accustomed to tradition that our offerings have become routine? Let's take the opportunity today to mindfully be present in everything we do. Let's look at the deeper meaning and offer it all to the Lord.

Be mindful as you go about your day.

True Justice

Render true judgments, show kindness and mercy to one another, do not oppress the widow, the fatherless, the sojourner, or the poor, and let none of you devise evil against another in your heart.

ZECHARIAH 7:8-10 ESV

Justice is the Lord's. We've heard this more than once throughout our lives. He is the one who keeps vigil for the vulnerable and who ultimately holds us all accountable to our actions. So, how do we practice the justice of God? Is it not to feed the widow, help the poor, and take care of orphans? That is mercy in action.

May we not forget how practical God's mercy is. When we show kindness to one another, without looking for excuses to withhold it from each other, we practice the law of love. When we are hospitable to the traveler and compassionate to those in need, we reflect the merciful kindness of God. Let's have hearts that seek true justice and do good to all. In so doing, our motives will remain pure before the Lord.

Offer practical help to someone in need today.

Mindful One

*When I consider Your heavens, the work of Your fingers,
the moon and the stars, which you have ordained,
what is man that You are mindful of him,
and the son of man that You visit him?*

PSALM 8:3-4 NKJV

When we realize how great and vast God is, how powerful, creative, and wonderful he is, it can almost be too much to know that he thinks of us. Though he knows the inner workings of every aspect of the universe, he is intimately aware of us. He knows us not just in theory, but deeply, truly, and compellingly. His love is overwhelmingly pure, and his mercy is mightier than the most explosive power the world has ever known.

Look to the heavens and try to count the stars. There are countless bright spots in the night sky. God knows each one and their size, material, and details. Not only does he know all the stars, planets, and galaxies, but he knows you. He thinks of you, and you are a delight to him! As you gaze at the sky, may you find that your heart awakens in wonder at this marvelous God who chose you as his own.

*Look at the stars. For every one you count,
remember that God knows you just as well.*

Defender

The LORD defends those who suffer;
he defends them in times of trouble.
Those who know the LORD trust him,
because he will not leave those who come to him.

PSALM 9:9-10 NCV

When we go to the Lord for help, he answers us. He shields us with the power of his presence and lightens our loads by putting the weight of them on himself. He takes our weakness and shows off his strength through us.

When we suffer, God comes to our defense. He meets us in the dirt when tears stream down our faces. He lifts us up and carries us through the thick of the battle. When we trust him, there is nothing to fear. He will not let us down. He never leaves those who come to him, and he will not abandon them to the fears that threaten their peace. His peace passes all understanding, settling our hearts even in the midst of suffering. May we press into his presence, knowing that he is closer than the air in our lungs. Our defender will not fail us.

Trust the Lord to fight your battles.

Good for You

It is good to give thanks to the LORD,
to sing praises to the Most High.
It is good to proclaim your unfailing love in the morning,
your faithfulness in the evening.

PSALM 92:1-2 NLT

Gratitude is more than a simple act in the moment. It builds an attitude of humility before the Lord that enables us to look for his unfailing love around us. There is not a single second where we don't have access to the loving arms of the Father. When we start the day looking for where his abundant compassion meets us, we open our eyes to the possibilities of his goodness all around us.

As the day winds down, we can recount the ways that we experienced his faithfulness with us through the day. How has God helped us when we needed it? A heart of thanksgiving lets us embrace the day for its opportunities because we know the Lord is the one who helps us through every problem. He is the one cheering us on to victory. It is good to give thanks to the Lord, so let's do it freely. With open hearts of adoration, let's sing praises to the one who is ever-present in loyal love and who faithfully leads us through each day.

Thank God for how he has specifically helped you.

King above All

The LORD is a great God,
and a great King above all gods.
In his hand are the depths of the earth;
the heights of the mountains are his also.
The sea is his, for he made it,
and his hands formed the dry land.

PSALM 95:3-5 ESV

As we consider the last year, the hills and valleys, the triumphs and the defeats, may we look through the lens of God's mercy. What has gone well? Where have we seen God move in ways that caused our hopes to soar and our hearts to swell? Where have we needed God's comfort and reassurance?

Through it all, how has the practice of gratitude contributed to your growth in the Lord? Has it helped your prayer life, your peace, or your relationships? Has it challenged your assumptions or helped you to let go a little easier? As you spend time reflecting over the year and its challenges, may thanksgiving fill your heart. May the Lord bless you and keep you as you look to his leadership in the coming days, weeks, months, and years. He is the same yesterday, today, and forever, and he remains the King above all!

Reflect over this last year and write down your key takeaways.